Why Did I Ever Get Married!

Amrita Sharma

Why Did I Ever Get Married!

1st Edition published in India by Vishwakarma Publications in April 2023

ISBN - 978-93-93757-92-0

Disclaimer

The views and opinions expressed in this book are the author's own and the facts are as reported by her, and the publisher is not in any way liable for the same.

Published by:

Vishwakarma Publications

34A/1, Suyog Center, 7th Floor, Gultekadi Marketyard Road,
Giridhar Bhavan Chowk, Pune: 411037, Maharashtra, India.

Mob.: 9168682200

Email: info@vpindia.co.in

Website: www.vishwakarmapublications.com

Cover: **The Book Bakers**

Typeset and Layout: **Vishwakarma Publications**

Printed at: **Spectrum Offset, Pune**

Dedication

To my dearest Anand and Ritu - for ever and ever

Acknowledgement

I WOULD LIKE to express my heartfelt thanks to Suhail Mathur of The Book Bakers literary agency, for believing in the book and making me part of the TBB family.

Many thanks to Vishal Soni, CEO, Vishwakarma Publications, for having found the book interesting enough to select it for publication; to my editor Sneha Bawari for her contribution; and also to Nupur Jain, Project and Rights Coordinator, Vishwakarma Publications for covering all corners and taking personal interest in the project.

The book would not have been possible without the support of my family – Mum, Dad, Ritu, Anand and my husband Keshav, who did full justice to his task of being the 'second pair of eyes'.

Most of all, my heartfelt gratitude to each and every one I interacted with regarding the book, for being open about their feelings, their experiences and their insight – all of which formed the backbone of my latest work.

PREFACE

"Love is blind but marriage is a real eye-opener."
– Pauline Thomason

ENTERING MATRIMONY IS not difficult; neither is getting out of it anymore. What is difficult, however, is staying married and that too - staying happily married.

Going by all the discussions at relationship forums, experiences with acquaintances, and some heart-to-heart conversations I have had with my close friends, I have realised one thing – that marriage, is very much like driving. You decide you want to learn driving, then you choose a trainer, learn all the rules by the book and by the time you collect your license, you feel you are all set for the road. You believe that since you know all the rules, nothing can go wrong. But driving, like life, is best learnt when you are thick in the process of driving. It is only when you are out there, in the chaos, in the maddening traffic, where you find to your shock that while you are going by the book and following all the rules, the car driver in the lane next to you is on his/her own trip. It is then that you realise that there is a vast difference between learning something and practicing it, between doing full justice to your own skills and paying for the lack of it, in the form of the fellow passenger on the road. It is then that you realise that no matter how prepared you are to drive, the real success of your driving skills lies in your ability to negotiate the chaotic traffic, minding the twists and turns, and managing the hairpin bends. It is how you go through the bumpy road that decides whether you survived the driving or pulled over and called it quits.

Many a married couple have complained that they had everything planned out but things did not turn out anywhere close to what they had expected. One speed breaker, one barricade or one wrong gear and the whole vehicle can go off balance – in some cases, even turn turtle. Likewise, starry eyed couples who started out with high hopes and expectations, sometimes find themselves feeling disillusioned, cheated, bitter and even miserable – and all because things did not turn out as expected.

It often leads me to wonder then, if we are setting our expectations for marriage really high? Is our idea of marriage and married life unrealistic? Are we plain unlucky in marriage, or are we all clueless about "marital arts"? Are we just fooling ourselves about love and marital bliss, or is it an enigmatic secret we have yet to decode?

In life, things are rarely in black and white; it's often shades of grey that we are faced with. Even in marriage, things may not turn out as we imagined, as we perceived, as we planned, but that's how life works. It's no surprise that most of all will agree with English-American comedian, Henry Youngman's statement – "*The secret of a happy marriage remains a secret.*" What we can do is to take things as it comes, go with the flow and work around roadblocks and hurdles to negotiate our way through the maze of married life. Sometimes, it only takes some skills, some alertness and some fortitude to stand our ground, not give in to divisive forces and make sure that you both give all you can to make things work. Maybe it turns out to be a different kind of reality, a different kind of happiness than the one you dreamed of or visualised, but the fact is, where there's a will, there is often a way. As long as both of you decide that no matter what, you want to stay together, be there for each other and work things out no matter what it takes, it is highly likely that there is, after all, a happily ever after.

Contents

CHAPTER 1

FROM DUAL INCOME TO SOLE EARNER

I HAD ALWAYS known Ajay and Shikha to be a very chilled out couple, and they were among a few couples I knew who had lots of things in common. They had been working in the same IT firm but in different departments when they fell in love and decided to get married.

In fact, meeting them belied the phrase I have often heard – 'opposites attract'. In their case, what brought them together was that they had too many things in common!

Both enjoyed eating out, partying, entertaining people and traveling to exotic places every now and then. That not only added to their compatibility but also helped them to spend a lot of 'quality time' together.

But since relationships are quintessentially dynamic, changes are part and parcel of its fabric. What makes this aspect so significant in terms of relationships is that no matter how 'sorted out' things are when we enter matrimony, one is thrown off guard when things change and one realises that the situation is not so 'sorted' anymore. This includes the employment status of the couple when they got married. As long as finances are taken care of, things work fine. But what happens when one of them suddenly loses her job and finances come under a cloud? Does the relationship take a beating because the monetary equations have changed? Does the status from dual income to single income take a toll on the relationship?

In this case, being a close friend of both Shikha and Ajay, I got to see how the graph of the relationship changed with the highs and lows of income.

Shikha and I were in college together but I got to know Ajay very well when she started seeing him.

Even after they got married, they continued with their extravagant lifestyles. Being financially sound, spending came easily to both of them.

Neither had any major responsibilities to take care of, which is why they could indulge a lot in eating out, travelling, shopping and even going ahead to buy a house. Since they shared the EMI, neither ever felt any pressure on that account.

But trouble started when Shikha started having problems with her boss, which began affecting her peace of mind.

"He would keep putting me down, insulting me and deliberately ruining my appraisals. Ajay was also aware of what I was going through and when one day things got too much, I told him that I wanted to leave. He agreed and said that he supported my decision," she said.

After she left her job, she started looking for another one. However, things were not going too well on that front. She started some freelance work, but it was nothing compared to what she had been earning. Soon it started taking a toll on their marriage, as they suddenly found themselves turned into a single income household from that of a comfortable dual income.

"It was unexpected and now obviously we had to be careful with our expenses. Our outings reduced drastically, our activities that we enjoyed together – such as going out for movies every week, dining out, going bowling or partying – all reduced and it started reflecting on the quality of our relationship. Now the only conversation we seemed to have, was about bills to be paid, groceries to be bought and what each of us considered 'worth' spending on," says Ajay.

For Shikha, it was equally traumatic since she was now in a position where she had to ask Ajay for anything or everything that was needed in the house.

"I was shocked at how he started snapping every time I told him about buying something. It was almost as if I was making it up or I was trying to put unnecessary burden on him. I suddenly felt that he had married me not for me but for the income I got home, which had made our lives so comfortable and extravagant," she said.

Counsellors admit that such a situation can affect a marriage severely and even push it to the edge. It's also very natural since when the couple started out, they had a certain framework in mind, within which they operated their life and their relationship. When that changed, the relationship is bound to change as well, they said.

I saw that in a similar case when my colleague Raghav got married to his family friend Gauri. They were also both high-flying professionals with glamorous jobs that entailed a lot of travel and fun. And then one day, due to a major tiff with the organisation's top management, Raghav put in his papers. It was a jolt to Gauri, who had a two-year old son and was thinking of planning another one.

She was quite worked up when she brought it up when we met for tea. She was in the same building for some work and we decided to meet up and chat.

"Suddenly I have had to put my life's plans on hold. All the things that Raghav and I had talked about have just gone down in the dumps. He refuses to talk about taking up another job, can you imagine? He says he is really put off by the whole episode and is now determined not to work for anyone anymore," she said, shaking her head.

I was at a loss of words myself.

"So, what does he plan to do now?" I asked.

"Well, he has made up his mind to start his own work. I don't think he understands that it requires a lot of capital and we don't have that kind of back-up," Gauri said.

Raghav, on the other hand, was unwilling to change his decision.

He was determined to work for himself and said he was hurt that Gauri did not support him in this.

"It's not like I don't want to work anymore, and it's not like I wouldn't be contributing to the household expenses from here on. But yes, I am aware that it would take time before my firm is established and I expected Gauri to understand that and stand by me. I know it has fallen on her to pay the bills and take care of the expenses, but isn't that what marriage is all about - to support the other when one needs it?" he asks.

Gauri, on her part, found herself completely in a position of disadvantage. It's not that she did not want to support Raghav at a time when he was out of job. What gave her sleepless nights was the fact that he wasn't intending to join back work at all.

"As far as he was concerned, he was through with taking up jobs. He was going to take his chances in life conveniently, putting the whole burden of providing for the house and our other expenses solely on me. I felt really let down by him and what was more. I started losing respect for him as a husband, as a partner and as a man," she says.

I was prone to questioning if respect was really related to the financial status of the partner, but I realized it was something else that was at play here. Psychologists say that respect for each other is not always about economics and finances. It's more about whether a person is capable of taking care of oneself, one's family, one's life and one's own needs. That is what forms the foundation of respect even in marriage. Any person, who conveniently offloads his/her burden on someone else, loses respect in the eye of the other! That is what couples need to guard against at all times, since respect for a partner is one of the main ingredients of a strong marriage.

In some cases, couples also deem it an act of betrayal and an act of cheating when one partner suddenly decides to opt out of the 'earning group' and sit it out.

This is what happened with Rishabh and Sonam. When they got married, they were both MBAs working with private firms and earning really well. Even though it was an arranged marriage, the two had found each other compatible since they were from a common field and had lots to talk about.

"I had made it very clear that I wanted a working wife. My parents had both been working and I had seen how smooth life was because of that, especially since the experience of bringing up kids was not something easy for one partner alone to manage. That's why I had been very clear that I wanted a wife who had her own career," says Rishabh.

But when five years later Sonam conceived, she had a tough time coping with the pregnancy.

Things came to such a point that she had no choice but to quit. Rishabh, who was not mentally prepared to take on parenthood single-handedly, became stressed out.

He had hoped that Sonam would re-join work as soon as the baby was born so that they could share the financial burden of bringing up a child but it had been over a year now and Sonam's break extended on and on. One day when Rishabh broached the subject, she said she had no intentions of going back to work now and that she wanted to spend time bringing up the child.

"I feel really upset and betrayed by her. How could she take such a decision alone? I had not bargained for this when I got married to a working woman. I was clear from the beginning that I wanted a double-income household, and she knew that. And now, just like that she has left me as the sole breadwinner. It is a responsibility I resent a lot," he said.

The sense of being left in the lurch, of being 'cheated' by the partner, soon began to take a toll on their marriage. There were constant arguments, bitter fights, bickering about expenses, especially regarding the child.

"I couldn't believe that he was counting every penny being spent on our own child, that he was resenting everything being bought for our child and every occasion that was being celebrated in our life. Suddenly he was this accountant who was busy maintaining a balance-sheet about everything in the house. It made me sick and disgusted to see his changed attitude towards me and our child just because I wasn't earning anymore," she says.

According to marriage counsellors, where such an attitude in marriage is totally unacceptable, the rationale behind it is something else and that needs to be understood. They opine that the resentment is not due to extra expenses but due to the fact that one partner has been put in a position where the burden of managing the expenses has been put on 'one' rather than 'on both', as had been planned earlier.

It is this shift from an agreed position that causes resentment in the partner who is left to take on the responsibility of being the provider involuntarily.

One can't help but wonder then: are marriages only about economics? Is there nothing more to it than being double-income providers? What about love, emotions and companionship?

Relationship experts say that such situations can be dissipated or avoided if the couples have an open communication about the issue. It is natural for people, for relationships, for partners to change with time as life moves on. But as a couple, it is imperative that decisions which affect their marriage and inter-personal relations be mutually agreed upon and decided.

The fact that Sonam decided by herself that she didn't want to work anymore, without talking about it with Rishabh, aggravated the situation between them. Marriage counsellors say that any issue that threatens a marriage, needs to be talked about. The institution of marriage is a joint venture and solo decisions are bound to be detrimental to its very existence.

Take the case of Kunal and Ishita. When Kunal was laid off from work he decided to go to the UK to look for a job on a friend's suggestion. But he first discussed it with Ishita. "I made sure that she and I were on the same page regarding my decision. Only after she agreed, I went ahead," he says.

It was almost a year when Kunal finally got a job, during which Ishita managed everything, including taking care of their son. "By that time, I was tired of my job and the company I was working for and the life I was leading. I just wanted to leave it all and join Kunal in the UK. I had managed it all for so long and I saw no reason why Kunal should object to my idea," she said.

But when she shared it with Kunal, she was surprised that he was hardly keen on it. "I had just begun; there was not much I could offer her at that time and I suddenly felt jittery that she who had a sure flow of income, was hell-bent on leaving that and relying on my meagre income of a beginner," he said.

It was a tough time for both and their marriage was under a lot of strain with the impending financial constraints. Both were experiencing a mixture of emotions – insecurity, apprehensions, fears, doubts, anger – at the whole gamut of change they were facing.

Counsellors say that it is often such phases that bring marriages to a make-or-break stage. It's crucial that couples handle such moments in their married life with their head not their hearts; with maturity, with composure and not make it an ego issue or a personal one. Since it is an issue that concerns both partners equally, it's best for them to work things out mutually and reach a consensus. Only then can the couples ride through this stumbling block.

This is what Kunal and Ishita finally did. One day, Ishita skyped Kunal and poured her heart out to him.

"I told him all that I was feeling, all that I was hurt about regarding his attitude and also that I knew the insecurities and doubts he had about my decision," she said.

On the other hand, Kunal confessed that he felt the timing of her decision was all wrong. "I told her that I loved her and would support her all my life. It's just that when I myself felt on unsure grounds career-wise, she at least should have held on till I was more settled in my new job," he adds.

And because they decided to communicate freely, they could also look for solutions together.

"I assured Kunal that once I came there, I would try and help him as much as I could and that he would not be left alone to fend for the family. I told him I would get a job really soon but I wanted to be with him, and not carry on with a job I despised so much. He was not very convinced but he agreed," she said.

Soon after she joined him in the UK, she managed to get a part-time job at a library. Within no time, she joined a course alongside and managed to get a TAship (teaching assistant) in the same university, which took care of their expenses to a great extent. Things were back on track and their marriage, which had almost reached the edge of a precipice, landed on firm ground once more.

Problems, insecurities and uncertainties are an integral part of relationships as life itself. What we begin with, is not often what we end with. And thus, it's important to negotiate issues, problems and disagreements by being open about it, by talking things over and communicating one's feelings. Once you understand that, then relationships can actually be salvaged before it is too late.

❍

CHAPTER 2

WHY 'DIRTY' CAN NEVER BE SEXY

I RECENTLY CAME across an unusual report in the papers about a woman from Madhya Pradesh filing for divorce on grounds that her husband shuns shaving and bathing for almost a week at a stretch.

At the outset it seemed amusing and one that would qualify for a list of 'unusual,' 'bizarre' or 'funny' reasons for divorce.

But in reality, it can be a deal-breaker as well, as seen in the case above.

When we meet someone for the first time, we notice how good or bad looking a person is, how stylish or classy or youthful looking the other person is, when it comes to external assessment.

One thing that hardly crosses our mind at such time is where he or she stands when it comes to personal hygiene. We almost assume that because a person is well-dressed, wearing branded clothes and sporting branded perfume, the person must be aware of how important cleanliness is.

But believe it or not, many newly-married couples have had a rude awakening because they discovered the 'dirty' side of their partners.

This is what happened with my friend Akriti. She had been dating Saurav for almost two years before they got married. But during the honeymoon period, Akriti got a shock of her life when she discovered her husband's smelly side.

"At first, I couldn't figure out why there was a stale smell in the room that almost bordered on stench. To my disgust, I found that my husband had this terrible habit of not changing his socks for days. He would wear them again and again till they were so dirty that they could not even be washed. He would then throw them away and wear the next set of socks for days again," she said.

"I felt miserable and even told him that his feet smelt, as did the whole room after he took off his shoes. But it made no difference to him, even though I told him that even the bed would stink," she added.

The worst part was that even though she told him that she couldn't sleep with him because the bed stank due to his dirty feet, it made no difference to him.

"For me, it was such a put off that I refused to sleep with him. That was what our first fight was about. There was a lot of tension but I stood my ground. Finally, he agreed to change his socks and our marriage was saved," says Akriti.

While Akriti was lucky that her problem could be solved, there are many such hygiene issues among partners that sometimes are very difficult to negotiate without the relationship being affected.

Something similar happened with my friend Mihir, who got married to Seema the arranged way.

Though their marriage had been fixed by common family friends, the two had ample time to meet and get to know each other before saying yes.

"What I was excited about was that we shared a good physical chemistry and I couldn't wait to sleep with her. She had an amazing figure and carried herself really well," recalls Mihir.

But he was in for a major disappointment when they got married and went for their honeymoon.

"The first time when we were about to make love, I found that she had such a strong body odour that it became impossible to touch her or stay close to her. I didn't know what to do and how to say that to her without embarrassing her. I made some excuse and postponed our lovemaking to the next day but it became a torture for me. There was no way I could feel aroused with that kind of body odour," he said.

Psychologists say that people do not attach much importance to personal hygiene, but what they don't realise is that the lack of it can impact a marriage in a drastic way.

"I finally had to tell her that it would be nice if she could bathe and come to bed since we both would be fresh to sleep together. I actually started having a bath myself at night so that she did not feel bad about it," he said.

It is not only the newly-married couples who face the hygiene demon. Sometimes, a partner starts demonstrating lack of hygiene over the years, as in the case of Rohit and Meera.

"Things were fine initially and our sex life was reasonably good. But with time I realised that he started neglecting his personal hygiene. He would often forget to brush his teeth and when we would make love his foul breath would take all the fizzle out of my senses. I just couldn't get in the mood," she said.

Soon that started affecting their sex life since Rohit would be annoyed with Meera when she lay there like a cold fish.

"I just couldn't bring myself to bear the breath, and I couldn't tell him either because I knew he would not take it nicely. As if that was not enough, I realised that on some days he would just slip out of his dirty underwear and slip under the sheets. For me, the thought that he was sweaty, dirty and smelly down there from the whole day disgusted me and the last thing I felt like doing was to be in bed with him," she confesses.

She started making excuses just so that she did not have to sleep with him on the days when he refused to bathe. "I dreaded the idea of having sex with him when he was not clean and coming down with UTI. I was paranoid about that," she says.

But her fears and her excuses did not help much. As a matter of fact, they ended up alienating Rohit from her.

Psychologists agree that such issues have the potential to complicate things between the couple.

When such instances of sexual rejection persist, the rejected partner starts feeling like he or she is being rebuffed. That not only creates a serious rift but is likely to damage things to a point of no return.

Experts feel that it is a good idea to talk things over if lack of hygiene is leading to a situation where the marriage might disintegrate, even though the unclean partner may not take it with a smile, so to speak.

But marriage counsellors strongly suggest that the rejecting partner must take the risk of letting the partner know: what and where the problem is. The risk of upsetting a partner is much less than the risk of losing him or her and breaking your marriage.

Even in this case, when Meera finally mustered up the courage to tell him that she just could not get in the mood because he had not washed up and she was uncomfortable about that, Rohit was deeply offended.

"I had to really make him understand that I loved him and loved making love to him, but I needed him to be clean and fresh so that I could stop holding myself back. For a few days, he was grumpy and even though he bathed, he refused to make love. But since now he was clean, I went out of the way to make a move and get him in the mood," she said.

It took time and effort, but it finally worked. Eventually, he realised that she was not rejecting him, since every time he bathed, he saw that she was a more-than-willing sexual partner.

I have also come across some couples who are into "we love each other for whatever and however, we are" – and that sometimes also means that once they get comfortable in their marriage, they give up taking care of their appearance and sometimes their hygiene.

One of my colleagues who had been married for almost eight years now, stopped getting herself waxed. When I asked her why she did not go for her usual parlour trips, she said: "Oh there's no need for all that now. We have been married for so long now that it doesn't really matter. We have seen the worst of each other."

But experts say that being married for long is no excuse for not being sexually attractive to one's partner anymore. Women still love it when their husbands look and smell clean and vice-versa. In fact, there have been times when many good marriages broke down because the partners stopped taking care of themselves.

Take the case of Shomit and Ruma. When they got married, they were both sexually active for a long time.

"Even when we had kids, barring a short period of time, we still enjoyed having sex with each other. But gradually, Ruma stopped taking care of herself," he said.

It was true. Ruma had her hands full with the baby, the job and the house and somehow had no time left to take care of herself. She started neglecting her personal hygiene by not taking care to get her hair trimmed; her upper lip seemed to be competing with her husband's moustache and worst of all she had stopped getting her pubic hair trimmed.

"I felt we had spent so much time together and that it did not matter anymore," she said.

But the fact is that it did, and it does.

"I just could not bear the idea of having sex, knowing that there was a proper bush down there. It made me wince and I just did not fancy the idea of making love," he said.

Things had come to a point where sex had become conspicuously absent from their married life. And it would have been dead and buried if Shomit had not brought it up when Ruma got dressed for a party once and looked stunning after a long time.

"I was shocked when he told me that I needed to get myself as clean as I used to be, since he still felt sexually attracted to me and wanted to continue making love to me but not before I got the bikini area cleaned. I was embarrassed to the hilt but I was also flattered that he still wanted to make love to me. The very next day I took an appointment and have never neglected to take care of my personal hygiene since then," she adds.

The more I listened to these people, the more I realised that there's more to personal hygiene than meets the eye (or nose).

When we take good care of our hygiene, it reflects the importance we attach to our partner; it's a way of showing we care about the partner enough to take care of our personal cleanliness because we value the intimacy one shares with the partner.

Rugged looks and appearance might seem sexy in romantic novels and movies, but in real life, personal hygiene is what brings true romance in marriage. So, remember, staying clean and taking care of oneself is the best and most valuable way of showing love and respect for the partner.

CHAPTER 3

WHEN BEDROOM TURNS INTO BORED-ROOM

IT'S COMMON KNOWLEDGE that sex is an integral and essential part of any healthy and committed relationship. This intimate act between two people is not just an expression of their love for one another but one that brings them closer together. In the modern-day urban world, where both men and women are financially independent and equal partners in the institutions of marriage, the lines between who takes the lead and who initiates the sexual act has also narrowed down considerably.

There is also a lot of emphasis on a healthy life and diet in order to boost the sex life. Several studies and research also go on to reiterate the benefits of a healthy sex life on one's emotional, physical and psychological well-being. I myself have come across several articles on how couples need to be uninhibited and more expressive in bed, if they have to fire up their sex drive.

But what do you do when your partner simply rejects the idea of experimenting in bed?

That is exactly the grievance my friend Nitya had with her husband. "I want us to try out new things and enjoy sex to the fullest. But he refuses to budge from his usual position. What am I to do? I can't go around looking for other partners to experiment with? Why can't he understand that it's him I want to enjoy with," she wailed.

Once I got over the awkwardness of the confession, I tried to look at the issue from both sides. "Maybe he is scared and anxious about it. Maybe he is not too sure about himself," I subtly started. "Scared? What is there to be scared about?" she said, her frustration with her husband spilling over.

"I mean, you know men sometimes have performance anxiety, don't you? When he realises your desire for experimenting in bed, he probably backs off fearing that he may not be able to perform as per your expectations," I went on, relieved to see that I had her attention. "Yes, that is quite a sensitive issue for men I know," she said, nodding softly. "Exactly. And sometimes they would rather go without some fun in bed than to deal with performance failure," I added.

She sat there in her own thoughts, assessing the situation and processing what I had just said.

"I think you are right. He is quite active sexually otherwise, but every time I get over excited and am really in the mood to try out new things, he just backs off. Now I think, may be because he is worried about pulling it off," she said, her eyes wide with her 'eureka' moment.

"So, what should I do? I don't really want to give up my fantasies and return to our usual act. I find that rather boring and unexciting," she scowled. "Well, you will have to be patient with him. I am not saying don't be sexually expressive. But you have to be careful not to weigh him down by what he may perceive to be your 'great expectations' from him in bed. Try and take him along with your plans; involve him in visualizing it," I suggested.

She seemed satisfied with the idea and said she would start working on it as soon as possible.

The absence of sexual intimacy between couples can be quite disturbing in marriage – at least for one of the partners, if not both.

One of the reasons why your man may not be okay with you experimenting in bed is that both of you have yet to reach that stage of being sexually comfortable with each other. You need to get to where you can trust each other with your sexual fantasies and get the other to participate in it with equal zeal.

Experts say that sexual trust is very important between romantic partners and unless you develop that physical rapport and chemistry, experimenting in bed may not happen.

In order to get there, one needs to communicate more with their partner and convey what he or she wants him or her to do and let him or her know when it's enjoyable. This will enhance sexual confidence and help understand each other's desires and pleasure points, and will lead to a chemistry that is not only mind-blowing but amazingly comfortable as well.

❍

CHAPTER 4

ALMOST UNFAITHFUL

IT ALL STARTED when I sat down to watch 'Unfaithful' - the movie I had heard so much about, and which also had the ever-suave Richard Gere and the delicious Oliver Martinez. As I sat down with a cup of tea in my hand, I was drawn to the gripping emotional drama that unfolded before me. It had everything – a passionate woman caught in the routine life, the 'good' husband (who sometimes translated to being a 'boring unexciting partner') and the unexpected rush of adrenalin in life in the form of a passionate lover who triggers off a whole chain of emotions – of unbridled passion, of lies and deceit, of infidelity, of breaking away from all that was familiar and dull.

But by the time the movie ended, I was not just left with the feeling of having seen a gripping movie, but also with a series of questions about relationships. As I sat down with myself, I couldn't help but ask – "what was it that made the woman drop everything that was safe, secure and loving, and led her to be drawn into a dangerous unchartered course when there was so much at stake?" Recently I met an old friend Shradha, who confided in me that she had bumped into an old flame, Rajan, and was now 'innocuously' meeting him every now and then 'just to catch up'.

I couldn't help but wonder if she was aware of what she was getting into. Was she even aware of the risks she was taking and of the repercussions? I was most concerned about the whole emotional upheaval she was exposing herself to.

And when I asked Shradha about it, she was as clueless as I was. But yes, what she was completely sure of, was that she couldn't resist – more importantly – did not want to resist!

"I know what you are saying. It is risky and sometimes, I must admit, it doesn't even feel right. I make excuses to come and meet him and we exchange messages and are constantly in touch, and my husband knows nothing about it. But it's not like I am sleeping with him. I just enjoy the thrill of it, the excitement and I think it's harmless," she said, making sure to not catch my eye. But the truth was staring at us both. We both knew it was not as innocuous as she said it was, and she also knew it very well. "I know you are judging me, but I don't think I am doing anything wrong," she said almost defiantly when I didn't say anything.

I had to tell her that I was no one to judge and it wasn't even my business to judge. "I am just concerned that you know the repercussions, if your husband finds out about this. If you think you will be able to make him understand you are not cheating on him by this 'innocuous' relationship, then there's nothing to worry about," I said. I had only echoed what she had spent days thinking about, which is why she let out a long sigh and nodded.

We both sat and discussed how a romantic relationship is different from a sexual relationship.

"I just like spending time with him, talking to him and sharing things about my life with him. He is very easy to talk to, very trust-worthy and I feel relaxed when I am with him," she said.

"I am sure. But your husband will not see it as that. In fact, he might feel more hurt and jealous and betrayed by the fact that you feel emotionally connected to someone else and not him," I noted.

"I know," she pressed her hand to her temple. "Why are relationships so complicated?"

She also told me about an incident when she was 'almost caught' by an acquaintance.

"I was in a coffee shop with Rajan and we were busy laughing at something he had told me when this neighbour walked in. I almost panicked. Before I could duck or run away, she spotted me and waved and started walking right towards us. I just about managed to keep calm and casually introduced Rajan as my second cousin, who was in town on some project," she said.

"Luckily, she bought it, also because Rajan very casually asked her to join us. Fortunately, she had come with her kitty party gang, and had to join them. But that was a close call. That's when I also felt I was playing with fire," Shradha said.

"Then why are you still in the same situation?" I asked, more out of curiosity than a reprimand.

"I don't know really. May be because it makes me feel alive, it makes me feel desirable and loved again, it fills my life with excitement, which somewhere along the way has vanished somewhere. I am not blaming my husband. It's just that with so many challenges to deal with, romance is the last thing we have time for. This whole affair with Rajan just adds that missing zing in my life and I feel I deserve to be allowed that much of pleasure," she said, vehemently.

May be that was her way of dealing with her life, her needs and her desires. Ultimately, each one is the best judge of what's at stake and yet if one is willing to take chances with infidelity – in whatever way or form or reasons, the truth is one has to be fully aware of the consequences – for you, for your partner and for your relationship - when you choose to walk down that path. Many of my friends have often debated this issue, saying it's their right to choose the people they want to be close with. Of course, it's their right and their choice. But then, we must also be aware of what's at stake and what we may stand to lose in the process.

This is the dilemma that one of my old friends, Vikram, faced. He met this woman in the park where he would often take his son to play. Puja would also be there with her son and the two started chatting since their sons were close friends. One day he saw her waiting for an auto when he was leaving for his office in his car. He offered to drop her and when he spotted her there the next few days as well, he offered to drop her every day since her office was on the way to his office.

But when he mentioned it to his wife, she was not very happy with his gesture and warned him against repeating it. While Vikram continued to drop her, he withheld the information from his wife. "I saw no point in complicating things. I enjoyed Puja's company. She and I would have a great time chatting and joking. She had a great sense of humour and I looked forward to the ride with her. I felt my wife wouldn't really understand and so there was no need for her to know," he told me.

But trouble started when one day Puja met his wife in the park and mentioned that Vikram had been dropping her off every day and she had often invited both of them for dinner, but he had never taken it seriously.

As expected, there was hell to pay at home.

"She was livid. I couldn't believe things would get so out of hand. She not only screamed at me but she also called Puja and warned her to stay away from me. It was so humiliating and disgusting," he said.

"But you must see it from your wife's point of view as well. You were hiding things from her and meeting another woman without her knowledge and what's more, you admitted you enjoyed her company. How can you not expect her to be upset?" I asked him.

"But there's nothing to it. I just didn't tell her because she wouldn't understand," he replied. I could only shake my head and leave him to deal with it. But I couldn't help but wonder how people can be blind to the impact of their actions on their relationships.

One partner's actions are bound to have an effect on the other and eventually on the relationship.

Relationships come with responsibilities as well, and a careless attitude can often end up in rocking the fidelity boat.

❍

CHAPTER 5

CAN THE REAL SPOUSE PLEASE STAND UP?

'REAL SPOUSE?' EXCUSE me, but is there anything like an 'unreal spouse?' Well, actually there is.

Besides the spouse we are married to, exchanged vows with, share our bed with, what if there is another person in the picture who gets the tick mark on most of the checklist that we associate a 'spouse' with?

He or she is the one we spend quality time with, share the account of the whole day in detail, hang out together, have common friends and topics and sometimes even travel together. What's most important is that the moment we have a problem, he or she is the person you seek – for help, for advice or to just vent out one's feelings to.

Now if that is not what an "ideal" partner should be, what else is!

Ladies and gentlemen, this person is none other than our special colleague and friend at work aka 'work spouse,' with whom we spend more hours than with our 'real' spouse.

So, what is it that makes work spouse so important in our lives?

"They understand you really well – they know exactly how you feel when things are going horribly wrong at work," says Rhea.

According to Rhea, she had a very tough time dealing with a nasty boss and unreasonable deadlines, and it never helped when she spoke to her husband about it. "He could never understand what I was going through. He would start giving me lectures and instructions on how to deal with my boss without any idea about the whole situation. That's when I happened to speak to one of my colleagues about it. And my god, I can't tell you how much that helped. He heard me out and knew exactly how I was feeling since we were in the same boat and could relate so well to the situation. Since then, I don't share a single word about my office with my husband. I can't wait to reach office, rush for a coffee break and vent my frustration to someone who I know understands me and my feelings completely," she says.

She is not alone in feeling so close and comfortable with the work spouse. In today's world, where men and women are increasingly working together and developing a strong bond – that is not necessarily romantic – is a phenomenon that has emerged and is here to stay.

According to Wikipedia, 'work spouse' refers to 'a co-worker, usually of the opposite sex, with whom one shares a special relationship, having bonds similar to those of a marriage.'

With such closeness and intimacy being an integral part of a relationship with work spouse, lines can sometimes get blurred between the two important people in our lives.

This is what happened with Vijay and Sheena. Both being lawyers, they would often get cases where they had to work together. Spending too much time, with such proximity and common interest led to the two becoming really close.

"Neither of us even thought of leaving our respective spouses but we could not bear the idea of spending too much time away either. We would look for excuses to work together, stay beyond our work hours just to get more time together, hang out together on the pretext of taking a break from work. The fact that I could talk to her about work, about my frustrations, about my ideas and she would listen to it all and share that important part of me and my life – made me really connect with her," Vijay said.

"Even at home, I couldn't wait to call her and share when I had something funny to say, or something crucial I discovered about the case or sometimes just chat up about a colleague. It was such a comforting feeling to have no preamble to talk about people and situations we have in common," he added.

"So, did it never occur to you that your wife may get jealous or insecure?" I asked. I was really curious about this new concept.

"I am sure she would have been. But she knew that Sheena was my colleague and we talked about work, which was a fact. In fact, she would often be around when I would be chatting with her. That way she knew that our conversation was all about the office, our colleagues, our boss and our office politics. She would also enjoy it and I think because she was aware of the content of the conversation and the fact that I was not really hiding anything from her, she never felt insecure or jealous. Once in a while, she would get angry about me spending more time talking to Sheena than with her, but that was more of a marital complaint than that of a wronged wife," he said and I couldn't help but laugh.

But while Vijay was lucky, he had a spouse who was not insecure, there are many who are not that comfortable with the work-spouses.

This is what happened with my friend Anisha. One day, while we were busy window-shopping, I noticed that she was very quiet. Since Anisha had always been a chatterbox, it was easy to discern that something was amiss.

"Is everything okay? You seem very preoccupied," I couldn't help but ask.

She gave out a long sigh and then sat down on one of the marble seats. I sat down next to her.

"I think Mahesh is having an affair," she said, and I was taken aback.

"What makes you say that?" I asked.

"Over the last few weeks, I have noticed that he finishes dinner and while I am busy wrapping things up he excuses himself saying he is going to the terrace for a smoke. I would not have noticed but he seems to be taking too long on the terrace. A smoke takes a few minutes but he is gone for almost an hour. And when I ask him, he says he was busy talking to a colleague," she said.

"Maybe he is indeed talking to a colleague," I said.

Anisha shook her head. Last week, I finished clearing things up quickly and decided to join him on the terrace. When I reached there, he was not smoking but busy talking on the phone and it was a woman on the other side. I could hear her voice loud and clear. When I asked him about it he told me there was a lot of office politics at play and he was talking to this colleague who is on his side and often gives him valuable information about things happening in the office," she said.

"And you don't believe him?" I asked.

"Of course not. I mean, even if he is talking to a female colleague and even if she is helping him with his office politics, the fact is he talks to her every day without fail. It's almost like he can't wait to finish dinner and chat with her. He has never seemed so excited to share things with me. And I feel really hurt that the time in the night when he should be with me, he is busy chatting with her," she said, her eyes almost welling up.

I sighed. I couldn't blame her for feeling the way she was. After all, even if there was nothing going on with that colleague of his, the fact was, he was paying more attention to her than to his own wife, and she was clearly resenting it. Sooner or later, it would have an impact on their relationship.

"Listen, I know how you feel. But from what you have told me, I don't think he is really having an affair. It could actually be just office gossip and friendship. I feel you should talk to him and let him know that it's not like you don't trust him, but you feel neglected by his behaviour."

Luckily, she agreed to give it a try.

But after I came home, I had a lot of food for thought. I couldn't help but wonder that in such a scenario, how does one safeguard one's marriage against a work spouse, who obviously is equally special – if not more - than the real spouse itself?

Of course, there are no hard and fast rules for relationships and we all know that. But there are certain things we can keep in mind and follow if we need to ensure that our work spouse does not cast a shadow over our real spouse.

(1) Make sure that your work spouse stays within the periphery of work life and work hours and does not spill over to your domestic life.

(2) Make it a rule to never share secrets about your marital life with your work spouse.

    Tomorrow if he or she were to leave the office and move out, you may feel guilty of betraying your real spouse's secrets to another.

(3) Make your real spouse meet your work spouse. With familiarity, the real spouse would realize that there is nothing to feel threatened about and would not end up constantly wondering, who is it you keep talking to?

(4) Make an effort to keep your spouse engaged about what happens in the office. That way he or she will not feel cut off from what you bond over with your work spouse.

❍

CHAPTER 6

IS BOREDOM CREEPING INTO YOUR RELATIONSHIP?

"LISTEN, IS BOREDOM a criterion for divorce?" joked Mita, a friend of mine recently. We had gone to attend the Book Fair and after strolling through counters and counters of book stalls and buying a number of books, had decided to give our backs some rest and sit down for some refreshing iced tea.

"Depends," I said, suddenly alert to the potential of this being a very interesting aspect of married life.

"On what? I mean, can't I just tell the judge that I am bored in my marriage?" she said, with mock seriousness.

"You can. But then he will ask you what do you mean by being bored – bored of him, bored with your marriage, bored with monogamy or simply bored in life," I retorted with equal seriousness.

"All of the above," she said. We both stared at each other for a second and then both burst out laughing.

We kept giggling about it off and on after that, but after she left, I couldn't help but ruminate later, over what she had said.

This question cropped up again and again in my mind when I was working on my book – "*What Did I Ever See in Him!*" especially in the chapter about taking people for granted.

Even at that time I had realized that in a relationship, there was a strong link between taking each other for granted and being 'bored'.

How, you may well ask, and my answer would be that boredom starts creeping into the relationship the moment we start taking the other for granted.

While at one level it's a good thing to take your partner for granted since it implies that you two are now well settled in, that there's a sense of ease and security in the relationship, it also threatens to lead to complacency between partners.

It reaches a point where each one stops noticing the other, stops being 'aware' of the other's importance in their lives.

Togetherness tends to become a 'habit' more than anything else.

And the moment we stop being 'aware' of the other, we stop working on the relationship.

At the risk of sounding clichéd, I would like to share that, "When we are constantly putting something into the relationship, it flows like a river and remains fresh, alive and dynamic; but the moment we stop doing that, the relationship becomes still, stagnant, like a lake – thus leading to 'boredom'."

"So, what do you suggest to get rid of the boredom bug?" she said, when we connected again.

This time I realized that she was not really joking.

"Depends," I said again and I could hear a long sigh on the other side of the phone.

"On what?" she asked again. We were going down the same route again.

"On the kind of marriage you two have," I said, and this time she lost patience.

"I am just asking you what I can do to get rid of this overwhelming feeling of boredom in our marriage. Please don't complicate things for me by your profound questions. In my bored state, I don't have the energy to decipher your puzzles."

I couldn't help but laugh.

"Alright. All I meant was that relationships are also like designer clothes. What works for one, doesn't always work for another. But never mind. What I would suggest is, sit down and recall all the things that the two of you loved doing together initially, and which you don't do anymore.

"Think about it," I said.

"Ummm, well we used to love going for movies a lot. First, we used to go every fortnight, then every month, then it came down to once every few months and now I can't even seem to remember the last time we went together for a movie," she almost sighed.

"Then that's what you two need to get back to. Since you both are fond of movies, getting back to watching movies together will bring back the quality time you two had once," I suggested.

"Hmm, that sounds like a good idea. I am going to try that soon enough," she said. I also told her to let me know if it worked.

Two weeks later she called and sounded elated.

"It was amazing. He was not so keen initially and gave me a long list of why he couldn't go, but I was adamant. I insisted first and then threatened him and finally he relented. But once we stepped out, he just changed. He played music in the car; we sang along and laughed – something we hadn't done for a long time. We enjoyed the movie as well – with the popcorn and the drinks, and had lunch outside as well. It felt like there was a spark between us all over again," she said, giggling like a teenager.

"I am so glad," I said, smiling at her joy.

"And you know what? He has already made plans to watch another film after two weeks and he seems more excited than I," she added.

"Great. Just make sure to keep doing these things together so that you both stay on the same track. As for me, I am glad that the judge will not have to hear takes of your boredom anymore," I said and we laughed heartily.

That's the thing about relationships. The graphs can change their course anytime, anyhow.

Sometimes it's a lot of hard work no doubt; but sometimes it just needs a bit of tweaking, a bit of alertness and a bit of conscious effort to add a bit of spice in our marital life.

And like I said, different things work for different people – or couples. While for Mita, rekindling their old routine of going to watch movies did the trick, for Neha, my other friend, something totally different worked.

Neha and Rakesh were a couple who had met at work and then started their own firm after they got married. But even though they spent the major part of their day together, they were only focusing on work and nothing else.

That's when Neha realized that boredom had become such a major part of their life together that it started affecting their marital life and their professional life as well.

"I started feeling disinterested in everything – especially with my husband. Every time he came to ask me about something related to either work, or even our kids or an important project, my instant reaction had become – whatever! I just felt bored of it all," Neha said.

That's when I realized that spending time together is not enough. It's spending "quality time together" that couples should focus on.

When she told me that she was seriously thinking of separating – at least for a while because she felt she was seeing too much of her husband and couldn't bear it anymore, I was taken aback.

Seeing my reaction, she had asked for my suggestion to salvage the situation.

I had shrugged and said – "I don't know. I mean it's about the two of you and only you would know what can help you ride over the boredom in your marriage. All I can think of is that you two should start doing something together that has nothing to do with work and something that both of you enjoy."

She sat there thinking hard and then suddenly jumped on my couch.

"I know what to do. I just got a leaflet yesterday about Zumba classes in the club nearby. I was thinking of joining it myself, but had no energy to do so. But I can ask Rakesh to join me, since he also loves to dance and is also into fitness," she said, excitement written all over her face.

She gave me a high-five and almost ran out of the house to rope her husband in.

It was only after a month that I got a call from her, inviting me to their firm's latest exhibition.

"Of course, I will be there. By the way, how's your Zumba class going?" I asked. Frankly I was quite curious to know if she had managed to coax Rakesh to shake a leg, since he had long been out of practice.

"Oh yes, we have been going regularly and I can't tell you, what a difference it has made to our lives. We can't wait to leave for our class and have started having so much fun that I am keeping my fingers crossed," she said, and I almost felt like hugging her because of the way she said it.

"Fingers crossed then. I am really glad to hear it. I will see you at the exhibition," I said.

But after I hung up, I couldn't help but wonder, how small things can have such a big impact on our relationships. In this case, I also couldn't help but recall an article I had read in 'Psychology Today' which said that recent research suggests that: 'Couples who sweat together really do stay together.'

The more I listened to my married friends, the more I realized that boredom seeps in very quietly – like age. And in order to keep boredom away from your relationship, it's important to keep experimenting, trying out new and different things – because ultimately boredom doesn't mean you are bored of the partner; it only means you are bored of the stillness that has crept into the flow of your relationship.

At times like these, you need to throw a stone or two to send some ripples through the stagnant waters of your relationship.

CHAPTER 7

ARE YOU FINANCIALLY INCOMPATIBLE?

"THE HANDLING OF finances is one of the major emotional battlegrounds of any marriage. Lack of Finances is seldom the issue. The root problem seems to be an unrealistic and immature view of Money." – David Augsburger, The Meaning of Money in Marriage.

Financial matters have been among the top ones in the list of contentious issues in a marriage.

Even when women were not working and were not financially independent, the subject of how much money was saved or spent was always a sensitive issue between couples.

But today, things have become far more complicated with both partners earning and managing finances. In such a situation, issues of transparency, honesty, clarity and consensus with regard to money matters, has become very critical to marital relations.

Problems regarding finances can be of several kinds, and may differ from couple to couple.

But one of the most common issues about money arises from different approach towards spending money.

Different approach towards spending

In a marriage, it's natural for partners to be different. They may like different things such as different food, movies, songs or even décor. But when it comes to difference in spending habits, things can get serious because the issue is often a 'sensitive' one.

Take the case of Arti and Mohan, who separated after four years of marriage because they couldn't cope with each other's approach towards spending.

While Mohan was very easy-going and liberal with spending money, to the point of being a spendthrift, Arti was a very careful spender, to the point of being tight-fisted.

"He would only think of himself, of the present and his friends and never spare a thought about our future, about me or even about the financial security of his family. It gave me sleepless nights the way he just splurged and spent thousands and thousands with his friends at a pub or on dinners," she complained.

His side was totally different from hers.

"I know how important it is to plan for the future and I have invested a certain amount which I feel I can manage with. But I can't put my present life on hold for a future which may or may not come. I have been brought up in a way where we like to live in the present. I am also not growing any younger. What about my desires, my wishes and my dreams to enjoy life while I still can?" he said.

They were both justified and entitled to their opinion and what for them comprised the 'right' way to live. But what didn't work for them was that they were not on the same page when it came to the issue of how, when and where to spend money.

Such different approaches to spending can lead to fissures unless the couple decides on a 'middle path' – where they have a consensus on 'how much expenditure is expendable'.

Different approach to investing money

One of the things that may never cross the couple while entering into a relationship is their approach towards investing their money. But believe it or not, like most of the contentious issues, different approaches to investing money can pose as big a threat to the relationship than any other.

Take the case of Maya and Ashok, who almost parted ways because they were on the opposite sides of risk taking when it came to investment.

While Maya was out-and-out conservative when it came to investing, Ashok was more of a risk-taker, which often led to serious fights between them.

"I am of the belief that investing in property will get us great returns, but Maya just wouldn't hear of it. I felt frustrated by her sense of insecurity in putting our money into what I felt was a good deal," says Ashok.

Maya, on the other hand, had a tough time dissuading Ashok from risking all that they had by investing in property, which would leave them with little liquid cash in their bank.

"Ashok was adamant about investing in CLP (construction-linked plan) but I felt we were blocking all our money in something which would take a lot of time to yield results. I preferred the safe investments in mutual funds and government bonds," she said.

Experts say that most of the time, how we approach risk-taking in investments reflects how we deal with life in general, and that's how the couples should deal with it. They add that it's not always about disagreements and egos but about our own insecurities and fears.

Counsellors' advice that an open communication about why we are in favour of certain investment plans and why against, can help clear the air between couples.

Once that is sorted out, it's quite likely that the couple will reach a consensus on how to plan their investments.

Take the case of Sufiya and Zain. When it came to investment planning, they realised they were completely at odds on the issue.

"I wanted us to invest in this amazing office plot my friend was selling but Zain was absolutely against it. He just didn't want us to touch our Fixed Deposits. I was furious at the opportunity we were losing," said Sufiya.

When things reached fever pitch between them, they decided to consult a counsellor.

"During the session I realised that Zain's fears of taking risk with money stemmed from his previous experience where his father had lost all their wealth in stock market. He just could not bring himself to take such risks with money. But when I understood his reasons, things became much easier to deal with," said Sufiya.

Counsellors suggest that the best way for couples to go about joint investment is to reach a common ground regarding risks to be taken. Once a couple reaches a consensus, then investments start yielding not just monetary returns but have a positive impact on the relationship as well. After all, when a couple shares investments, they share trust, risks and a future together.

Withholding of financial information

Sometimes couples also withhold information about their financial position and accounts, which can also pose a threat to their relationship.

With more and more couple having their individual careers and finances, it's common to have separate bank accounts. There's no harm in that. In fact, it saves both a lot of confusion. But what complicates matters is when one partner hides (a) one's income, (b) one's investments including shares, stocks and mutual funds, (c) one's bank account.

This not only leads to hurt but also results in lack of trust between the partners.

Take the case of Manish and Umaira. When they met, they were both well settled professionally and each one would handle their own finances, look after their tax returns and investments.

Umaira continued to do the same after they got married, but she shared all the details with Manish - about how much she earned, where all she had invested and how much money she had in her account.

In fact, they also worked out a common budget, where they contributed according to their earnings.

But once when Manish met with an accident and they needed more money than the insurance provided, he revealed that he had made several investments, from which he could withdraw to pay the bills.

"It came as a relief to me that he had that kind of money and we didn't have to ask anyone, but what hurt me was that he kept it from me. I felt that even after being in such an intimate relationship he could not trust me, then it's a sign that things were not right between us," she said.

Experts say that in such cases, trust is the biggest casualty. When one keeps financial secrets from one's partner, it is reflective of trust deficit in the relationship.

"I thought if she came to know about every penny I had, she would start indulging more, or start expecting more, and somehow, I felt safer that I had some money saved for a rainy day, or maybe if things somehow went wrong between us. I guess I was just safeguarding my interests," he admitted.

But no matter what the reasons are, the outcome is the same when such issues come out in the open - hurt, resentment and erosion of trust.

Lying about financial transactions

Similarly, when couples lie to one another about their financial transactions, it amounts to the same thing - lack of trust.

Take the case of Mira and Tarun. When the two got married, Tarun's finances were an open book. Mira knew about each and every account, investment and even the monthly amount he took out to spend on himself.

She had done the same - but not completely. She had some skeletons in her financial closet.

Her brother, who suddenly suffered a huge loss in his business, needed money and asked Mira for it.

She did give it to him but without her husband's knowledge.

"I just felt embarrassed about the situation because my husband had not really been in favour when my brother had taken the decision to leave his job and start his own firm. And I was also slightly fearful that he might ask me not to lend him any money. I was going to do it, irrespective of whether Tarun was fine with it or not, but I just didn't want to take any chance. It is my money and I can give it to anyone I like. But if he had not been in favour, it would have led to serious conflict between us. That's why I decided to keep it from him. What he doesn't know will not hurt him," she argued.

But the fact is, if and when, he was to know about it, cracks would be there, and more often than not, it's irreparable, because it's a matter of trust.

Counsellors concur that the area of finances is a very sensitive issue between the couple and which is why most couples steer clear of what may potentially turn into an area of conflict and tension.

But then again, playing the ostrich also doesn't work in this situation. The only way out is transparent and honest communication between the partners about the money.

There was a time when having joint accounts was an embodiment of mutual love, trust and harmony. But today, things have changed. It's far easier to manage one's own accounts and plan one's own expenditures by oneself than together.

But what makes all the difference is that both partners are not only clear about their financial dealings but always in the loop as well. This not only helps build mutual trust but minimizes the chances of misunderstandings, hurt and eventual breakdown of the relationship itself.

❍

CHAPTER 8

BED MANNERS OF SLEEPING PARTNERS

HAVE YOU EVER encountered a situation where you woke up in the middle of the night and realized that your partner has pulled the sheet off of you and is happily snoring away, leaving you exposed and shivering?

Have you ever had a major argument about the decibel of your partner's snores? Or have you ever had trouble sleeping because your partner is watching a football match with 'ouch' and 'yes' coming out every now and then, oblivious to your sleeping routine!!!

Well, welcome to the real world of not-so-romantic phase of your life.

Agreed that there was a time when the idea of "sleeping together" was one of the most romantic things for a couple in love.

And why not!

Sharing a bed actually reflects a sense of intimacy that most couples value. The sex, the passion, the orgasm - all of it make the idea of 'sleeping together' one of the most important perks of being in a relationship and being married.

But what happens when the sleeping partners start displaying sleeping patterns that are completely at odds with one's own?

Well, to begin with, it's almost the beginning of the end of romance - and may be eventually even the relationship.

You think I am kidding?

Well, take the case of Ashu and Kamal. When they got married after a long courtship of eight years, they had no idea that it would take just eight months to drift apart.

But the trouble started where they were least expecting it - in the bedroom!

When they were dating, they had no idea that the 'bed manners' of their partners could pose a threat to their romance.

But it came as a rude awakening to Ashu, who was just not a morning person, while Kamal was in the habit of waking up really early.

"Kamal would wake up so early that he could give the rooster a complex. And as if that wasn't enough, he would make no effort to keep the noise low. He would open and shut the bathroom door loudly and I could hear him gargling away and all his other ablutions loud and clear. My sleep was totally disturbed and even though he would leave for his morning walk after that, I could just stay in bed but was unable to sleep after that," she complained.

Because of lack of sleep, she would feel groggy, tired and therefore irritable the whole day.

"I tried telling him to keep it quiet but he just ignored it," she fumed.

Kamal on his part found it very difficult to deal with the situation.

"I have to wake up early since I am a morning person and I have been going for my early morning run since I was in college. I just can't change my routing suddenly. And I do try and keep it quiet, but how is it possible to brush my teeth, gargle and use the flush without making any noise?" he asks.

"It's not just the bathroom noise! It's also his alarm which keeps going off. The first time it rings, my sleep is disrupted. He then puts it on snooze and goes off to sleep. And I keep waking up all the times it goes off. While he happily walks out for his fresh air and health regime, I am the one left sleep deprived!" she said.

"This is too much. How can I wake up without the alarm? I call this unnecessary provocation. If she wants us to sleep in separate rooms, why can't she just be clear about it? I can handle that, but not this looking-for-an-excuse-to-fight attitude!" he retorts.

While both felt the other was in the wrong, the truth was that it was the relationship which was in the dock. Soon the so-called innocuous issue started spilling over into their relationship itself.

Soon they were bickering over anything and everything, and at night, sleep seemed to be the last thing on their mind.

Experts say that very often when couples start fighting over small issues, there's more to it than meets the eye.

According to them, the trigger may be one thing, but the deep-seated resentment may be the driving force of the constant fights.

Similarly, Vijay and Mohini also found themselves struggling with bedroom issues - in this case 'snoring'.

"At first, I didn't say anything because I felt uncomfortable telling him about it," she said.

Theirs was an arranged marriage and Mohini was not that comfortable initially with making this known to Vijay.

But soon, things started getting out of hand, because Mohini realized she couldn't sleep at all and was unable to cope with next day's work because of lack of sleep.

"When I told him about it, he almost blew up. He said it was not possible and that I was lying and just looking for an excuse to berate him," she said.

The issue not only led to the marriage turning sour, but also strained the ties between two families.

"I couldn't believe his reaction. What was so objectionable about it? It was a medical problem and he could have just seen a doctor for help," she said.

I have come across several articles which actually said many people have 'Resorted to divorce citing snoring as a reason.'

At first, I thought it was quite funny. But the more I heard about it, I realised it was anything but.

Counsellors also feel that the issue gets blown out of proportion because of the way it is handled.

"You should see the way she screams at me in the night and in the morning for snoring. First of all, I don't believe her, and even if I were to, it's not like I am doing it on purpose," he said.

To be fair, I am sure it makes the affected partner upset.

After all, there's nothing like a good night's sleep. And if that is affected, it is natural for one to be resentful.

But is screaming and raising a hue-and-cry the best way to handle it?

Not really. Experts say that it should be brought to the partner's notice very casually - without insinuating that there's a problem.

This is what Nisha did when she found out that her husband snored at night. After tossing and turning for days she realised that by pushing her head under the pillow she was actually pushing the problem under the carpet - and not really succeeding.

"I told him very calmly one morning that it seemed like he was in some kind of pain because he made some noises. He was alert and asked if he was snoring. I pretended it was no big deal but suggested he should see a doctor since it may be a result of some nasal block and may cause him further discomfort. He agreed and I quickly booked an appointment. He has been on medication and his snoring has improved as well," she told me with a wink.

And in return all I could say to her was - hats off, for winning the battle without firing a single shot!!!

This brings me to the point of ego. Many issues between couples sometimes get derailed because it becomes an ego issue.

Take the case of Nina and Vikram for instance.

Their relationship almost reached breaking point because of the television in their room.

While Nina worked in a school, she had to leave early in the morning because of which she preferred to crash early.

But Vikram, who worked as a journalist, had flexible hours and most of the time left for his office little late. He enjoyed watching TV till late in the night and that became a problem for Nina.

But when she tried to tell him to switch it off, he first scowled, then started grumbling and eventually refused to comply.

"I don't have to get up early so why should I pack up and tuck myself in so early? Please. I am not a school-going kid and she is not my Mommy who can tell me when to watch TV and when to switch it off," he said.

Nina, on the other hand, was shocked at his attitude.

"I can't believe how selfish he can be! Can't he see that I have to wake up so early? He can keep sleeping for the next four hours after I leave, but I don't have that luxury," she said.

When she told him to watch TV in another room, he refused.

"Why should I move? It's my room as well, and I like lying down in my bed and watching TV.

That's my way of de-stressing. As for her, she also comes back home by 4, and then sleeps for good two hours. Do I complain about that?" he argues.

The problem, which could have been worked out by proper communication and discussion, becomes critical because it is now a clash of egos.

Counsellors say that the moment ego takes over in a relationship, the resolution of the issue takes a backseat; scoring points over the other becomes paramount.

This is why they suggest that a confrontational approach should be avoided in such sensitive cases. The focus should be on conflict-resolution and for that the couple needs to sit and talk it out calmly without hurling accusations at one another.

Blowing hot or cold

Sometimes one is amazed at the small issues that get so big that they pose a threat to the relationship itself.

Who could have thought that something like the temperature of the air conditioner in the room can lead to a short-circuit in the relationship itself! But this is what happened between Vritika and Mahesh.

Come summers and the cold war would begin between them.

"He knows that I feel really cold in the AC but that makes no difference to him. No matter what I tell him, he refuses to increase the temperature. I feel miserable throughout the night, shivering and feeling uncomfortable, but he doesn't seem to care. I think that's just insensitive," she complained.

Mahesh, on the other hand feels the same way, accusing her of 'insensitivity'.

"Tell me one thing. If she feels cold, she can wear warmer clothes to bed and even take a thicker blanket. But if I feel that it's not sufficiently cold, what am I supposed to do? Sleep nude or what!" he retorts.

Counsellors admit that the thermostat issue can very often heat up things between partners - to the point where the relationship turns chilly.

To warm things up, counsellors suggest that couples must talk things over and find a mean method when it comes to room temperature.

The temperature can be set at a level which ensures that the room is not too hot and not too cold either.

After a session of counselling, Vritika and Mahesh decided to give things a try.

"I told her to set it at whatever temperature she wanted to, but then I saw she started wearing socks to bed and taking a thicker blanket, while I made sure the temperature was never so low that it affected her sleep," he said.

Winning a point may make a partner feel a victor and one who scored in the battle for power, but ultimately, it's the relationship which is lost.

Sometimes, a bit of understanding and empathy is all it takes for couples to arrive at a compromise - by choice. It's okay to cede some ground to the partner once in a while. After all, who doesn't need a comfortable room temperature - and a relationship as well!

❍

CHAPTER 9

IS YOUR RELATIONSHIP 'ALL WORK AND NO PLAY'?

ARE YOU TOO tired to 'just relax and chat' with your partner once you are back from work? Do you find it difficult to talk about anything other than work with your spouse? Are you spending too much time looking at office mails and messages than with your partner?

Do you get irritated with your partner's chatter when you are home from office? Do you just want to hit the bed and sleep when at home rather than stay up and spend time with your partner?

If you have said 'yes' to most of the questions above, then the verdict is that your work is affecting your relationship big-time.

In today's world, working couples are more of a rule than an exception. Both partners have their respective careers, their goals and their expectations as well, and since double income is more of a necessity than choice, couples often immerse themselves in their work.

After all, with both the partners earning, the possibility of a great and happening life becomes a reality. Own house, foreign trips, latest gadgets, latest model of cars, fine dining and socialising - all become a reality.

The flipside, however, is that with too much focus on work, relationships often take a beating.

Most couples find themselves spending less time with their spouses and more time at the office.

In such a scenario, while they end up thriving professionally, their personal lives leave a lot to be desired.

Take the case of Mahesh and Tanya. Their marriage almost broke down due to Mahesh's extensive focus on his career.

"His work required him to travel a lot and he would be gone for days. I had to be by myself for long periods and it didn't bother him that we hardly spent time together. I started feeling unwanted and unloved and finally told him I want out," she said.

"I couldn't believe when she said she wanted to separate. I mean, I felt I was doing all this for her - for us! I thought we were both fond of the good life and with the kind of money I earned, we were able to indulge. It came like a jolt from the blue when she said she was really unhappy with our life, with our marriage," Mahesh said, still reeling under the shock.

Counsellors say it is very natural for partners of workaholics to feel estranged from their spouses.

There is also a possibility of deep resentment setting in and eventually so much distance creeps in that it becomes difficult to bridge.

Sometimes, there is also a lack of awareness about how much is too much with regard to the time one is giving to one's office work.

This is what happened with Myra and Vinay. When Myra was promoted to the post of a Project Manager, she found herself handling a team of about 30 people. With deadlines, team issues, work pressure, she found herself constantly on her phone or laptop - sometimes even waking up at nights to check the progress.

Soon it started affecting her marriage. Her husband felt neglected since she seemed to pay more attention to her office than to him and their children.

Before she realised it, the distance between the couple had become so much that they lost the ability to communicate.

"We just stopped talking. It was only about the basic needs and what I was hurt about was, she didn't even notice. The fat pay cheques and the adulations had become so important for her that she failed to notice that she was losing us," he said.

It's true that it's not easy to keep personal and professional lives apart anymore. They seem intertwined to such an extent that it takes a lot to keep them separate.

But some couples find themselves so overwhelmed by their professional life that they unconsciously start putting in too much of their time, thought and energy into work. Before they realise it, their professional life has completely taken over their personal life.

When Nishant and Diksha joined work, they were both very clear about what they wanted from life.

But when her company started laying off people, Diksha started putting in a lot of time and energy into her job.

Though she managed to retain her job, she continued to be stressed out by the amount of time and energy she had to put into it.

Soon it started taking a toll on their marriage. Nishant started feeling neglected and ignored, as Diksha started focusing more on cementing her position in the office.

"She would come home late and then have a quick meal and start working on her laptop again.

We barely spoke and our sex life was down in the dumps since she was always tired. I started feeling like I didn't matter to her at all," said Nishant.

Diksha, on the other hand, was so pre-occupied with her work that she failed to notice her marriage failing.

Being under the kind of stress she was in, the two would often end up fighting and before they knew it, things came to a point where the two could not hold a decent conversation.

It's very common for partners to snap at each other or take out their anger and frustration on one another - for the simple reason that they are around and they can serve as a punching bag most of the time. But to counter such a situation, which will naturally arise, couples need to constantly communicate with each other.

Experts say that it is important for couples to realise that personal life is as important as professional life and maintaining a balance between the two, is crucial.

This is why they advise the couples to discuss openly the stress they are under, so that there is no misunderstanding or any displaced feeling of neglect.

It's also a good idea to ensure that the couples draw a line between their work life and personal life. For this they need to work out ways to spend time together – go on a vacation, go for a walk, participate in shared activities – so that both partners feel they are important to each other.

Counsellors advise that professional life should not seep into personal life to the extent that there is nothing left to hold a marriage together. They suggest that once home, couples should shut out the office work and focus on each other.

It's easier said than done, but then it's worth the effort.

❍

CHAPTER 10

QUALITY TIME- WITH YOUR SPOUSE OR SOCIAL MEDIA?

IT WAS MY ex-colleague Tanya's eighth wedding anniversary and of course I called her to wish her as soon as I remembered.

"So, madam. What plans do the love birds have for tonight?" I asked casually.

"Well, we hardly had time to discuss our plans, since Sunny came home from work quite late and I left home early today for office," she said.

"I hope you at least wished him," I said.

"Frankly, I didn't. He was still sleeping when I left. But he has wished me big time – on Facebook. He has posted about a dozen messages wishing me a happy anniversary, and they are so sweet," she drooled.

It was surely not my kind of sweet, but then you know what they say – to each his own!!!

"Great. So are the two of you going out or planning a cosy dinner at home," I asked.

"Well, I think I may be going out for dinner to this new fancy resto-bar that has just opened – at least that's what Sunny's Facebook post says," she replied with a bit of amusement in her voice.

Sunny was one of the most regular people on social media that I knew. Many times, I had felt that he almost lived his life on social media – posting pictures, links, videos and tweets on all kinds of platforms.

"Has he posted his plans on social media?" I couldn't help asking.

For someone not too active on social media, it was slightly incredulous for me to gulp that down.

"Oh yes. Just read his post. He said he will pick me up from office, and then he plans to take me shopping – to buy me whatever I like – and then take me to this new place for my favourite Chinese food," she said.

"Oh, how nice. I hope the two of you have a great day ahead," I said.

I didn't really have to wait to speak to her to know how the evening, the shopping and the dinner went.

When I logged on to my Facebook a few days later, it was all there – the heart-shaped pictures, the all-too-loving messages and new set of vows being exchanged on social media – with all of us as 'virtual witnesses'.

With so much of SMDA (social media display of affection), one naturally assumed that theirs was one of those 'marriages made in heaven' cases.

And so, when a year later I heard from another colleague that they were filing for divorce, I was stunned to say the least.

What could have gone wrong I wondered? Things had been going so well!!

But a few months later when I bumped into her at a mall and we sat down for coffee, it all came out.

She found out that he had been 'seeing' many women on social media for a long time and she actually, caught him one day when he went to the washroom, leaving his chat open, and she returned home while he was still in there.

"He had been chatting with not one but four of them! And it was pretty hot stuff. I felt so disgusted and angry and cheated!" she said.

Experts say that social media may have helped people stay connected, but it has also opened up a whole new world of communication with strangers, which ends up affecting relationships beyond repair, if partners don't know where and when they cross the line.

These days several researches are being undertaken to study the impact of social media indulgence on relationships. Marriage counsellors are also beginning to highlight the direct correlation of social media and breakdown of marriages.

The reasons for such concerns are many. Excessive use of anything is seen as an addiction.

When it involves something like substance abuse, one can see a doctor or get into rehab centres.

But when it involves a couple, addiction to social media can have a direct impact on the very survival of their marriage.

Take the case of Maitri and her husband Kaushal.

The first time she realised there was a problem with her marriage was when she observed that Kaushal never grumbled when she stayed in the other room working late into the night.

"I would often feel guilty because the work load used to be so heavy and with promotions round the corner, I would often end up working till really late in the night. We hardly got time together at night. But then I noticed that he would also be up till late. At first, I felt it was his way of supporting me and giving me company, but then I realized that he didn't really miss me because he was way too preoccupied on social media," she said.

Trouble started when even after she got free from work, he continued spending more time on social media than with her.

"I realized that we were hardly spending any time together anymore. He would be sitting right next to me, but would be laughing away, smiling away and busy posting comments on either Facebook or Twitter. When I ask him about it, he actually brushes me aside and gets busy tapping away on Instagram or Twitter. At such times it feels as if unless he comments, the universe will collapse," she said.

I laughed and she started laughing with me, but the truth was that beyond a point, it's not really funny.

"I can see he is more involved with social media than with me," she said.

While she said this in jest, the truth is, such a scenario has become more a rule than an exception today.

More and more counsellors are hearing from couples who feel that their marriage is suffering due to their partner's addiction to their gadgets and social media.

This is what happened with Madan, whose wife Asha had become a mobile phone addict.

"She is perpetually busy on WhatsApp. I see her buried into her phone, constantly tapping away messages, or busy sending forwards all day long. She has joined several WhatsApp groups – those of the women in the building, those from mothers from our son's class, those of her extended family, then those from her Yoga group and many more," he adds.

"What is most annoying is that even after I come home from office, she is busy checking her messages, forwarding them and playing endless videos. I have come to resent the fact that she hardly has any time for me and all her focus is on her phone and her WhatsApp messages," he further says.

Madan is not alone in this. Today, many couples are finding a great companion in virtual world than with their own partners.

There are smart phones, I-Pads, laptops, games, tablets, notepads that are serving as good substitutes for spouses.

Like Madan, Aditi had a similar story to share about her husband, who she says is a 'gadget Freak'.

"Every weekend I look forward to spending some quality time with my husband but it really upsets me when he sits with his video games and plays endlessly," she says.

She was not alone in her experience. In one such bizarre incident, one woman left her husband because he stopped helping with chores and paying bills – and all because he was obsessed with the computer game 'World of Warcraft'!

When I hear such cases, I can't help but feel that when Cupid unleashed the power of love and passion, he must have had no idea that the 'mouse' in the highly-technological world today will nibble away at the good-old version of romance.

I have actually heard many people say that they can fight and tackle a flesh-and-blood rival; but what can one do when one is pitted against social media and fancy gadgets?

Today, this actually seems to be happening with gadgets actually taking precedence over the partner itself.

This is what happened with Anya and Mayank.

When the two went on their honeymoon, Ayesha was more excited about clicking their pictures and posting them on Instagram. He went along with her obsession for a while but then lost his patience.

"I told her it was either me or the phone. We had a showdown and we both sulked throughout our honeymoon, but I just couldn't take it anymore that her public display of our time together was more important to her than actually being together," he says.

It's indeed sad that the need to share one's experiences on social media platforms has become so important today for most people that the concept of 'living in the moment' and 'creating memories' has taken a backseat.

This also brings to mind a recent incident where a couple from Saudi Arabia got divorced because the bride posted Snapchats at their wedding.

Another dangerous place to be is when couples bid goodnight to their gadgets and friends on social media before going to sleep rather than their partners.

In the 'good old days' couples would lie in bed and talk about their day, share their experiences and communicate with one another for hours.

But today, as soon as they get into bed, each one sits down with their own gadget – laptop, MacBook, iPad or even a smartphone – and starts a virtual interaction with hundreds or thousands of virtual 'friends'.

What each one pays no attention to, is the 'real' partner, in 'flesh and blood', sitting right next to them. This, becomes the first and the most severe casualty of social media fanatics.

And this is exactly what happened with Maitri and Jayesh, who had been married for four years.

"He was obsessed with checking Facebook and Instagram the moment he came to bed. And he would be at it, till he finally called it a night. He would barely talk to me, or listen to what I was saying; all his attention would be focused on what he should post on social media, how many likes he got and what were the comments about," she said.

One day, Maitri couldn't take it anymore. She actually burst into tears and yelled at him because she had been feeling really neglected.

"I told him that there was no point in staying together if all he needed from me was to share the living expenses. I told him he was too selfish and insensitive for making me feel like I was invisible and all he could see was the 'friends' on Facebook, Instagram and Twitter."

Jayesh on the other hand, felt she was just over-reacting because he couldn't believe that she was feeling 'jealous' and threatened by social media.

"That fool couldn't understand that I was not upset about his 'friends' on Facebook, whose attention mattered so much to him. I was upset about the time he spent on social media with his 'virtual friends' instead of the flesh-and-blood partner next to him who might want some of his attention too," she said.

For some time, Jayesh did back off but his withdrawal symptoms got the better of him and soon he was back to checking his Facebook, his news feeds and his Instagram followers before switching off the lights and that's when Maitri decided to call it quits.

Experts do say that social media addiction may not be the only reason for divorce, but it definitely can turn out to be one of the key reasons for the split.

That's because such addictions point towards deeper issues in the marriage. It could be due to lack of communication between the partners, incompatibility, and lack of sexual chemistry or may be something as simple as not being in love anymore.

But whatever the case, a marriage which breaks because of displaced attention – and that too to an inanimate rival – feels most frustrating.

Counsellors say that couples must never underestimate the importance of personal contact and interaction, especially in intimate relationships. Technology and gadgets can act as appendage, but not be a substitute for relationships. That's why it is vital that couples set clear limits on the time to be spent on social media and also on gadgets. If they are not careful, technology and gadgets can actually turn into monsters that will end up devouring the relationship itself.

That's why, the one thing that couples must never lose sight of – is the power of 'together time'.

It's only the time spent together that can serve as the bond between the partners and stand them in good stead in face of storms – even if it happens to be a social media storm.

❍

CHAPTER 11

NO KIDDING: TO HAVE OR NOT TO HAVE CHILDREN!

WHEN MY FRIEND Sneha got married to her colleague Rajdeep, both seemed like they were in seventh heaven.

They had decided on which house to live in, what furniture to buy, where to go for their honeymoon, how to manage their expenses and practically everything that ensured a smooth marital life.

The only thing neither thought of checking was the one thing that ultimately posed a big threat to their marriage itself. And that was the big question which had never occurred to either of them to ask – to have or not to have kids.

But after three years of marriage, when Sneha mentioned that they should start planning a child, he plainly refused to have one.

He said he had never said anything about having a child and if she had wanted one so badly, then she should have checked with him first, because he was 'just not keen on having any kids of their own'.

For Sneha, it was nothing less than a bolt from the blue.

"Isn't it obvious that once we are married, we would have our own family? What was there to ask? Isn't that natural? Isn't that normal?" she asked, unable to absorb the shock.

Rajdeep on the other hand, denies any wrongdoing on his part. He feels it was, in fact, wrong on Sneha's part to assume his choice on the issue.

"When did I ever tell her I wanted kids? Did she ever talk about it? If she assumed, then it's her problem, not mine," he said.

"What is there to assume! I mean, if having kids is the norm, it's the norm. If he didn't want kids, that is an exception and, in that case, he should have told me about it," she said.

She also gave her reasons for assuming what she calls the 'obvious'.

"When we were dating, he would love to play with his niece and nephew and I often saw him smiling at kids passing by, so I assumed that he loved kids. And now when I want to plan a family, he says he will not hear of it. What am I supposed to do! I feel terribly cheated," she says.

There were reasons for Rajdeep to stand his ground, but that did not help provide any solution.

As a child, Rajdeep had gone through a troubled childhood. With his parents divorced and he and his sister shunting between two houses and parents, the idea of having a child gave him the shivers.

"I had no inclination to bring a child into a world where there was so much uncertainty about how life would turn out," he said.

But that didn't really help the situation, since Sneha was enraged that his decision and his choice was affecting her life as well.

"How could he take a decision about a child that would not just be his but mine as well? I felt betrayed and hurt by his whole attitude," she said.

It is at such times that the dilemma of choice engulfs the relationship – whether to accept things the way they are or call it quits because the partner wants different things from life.

When I first heard about it, I was both shocked and amazed.

If the issue was so big and had the potential to make or break a marriage, then how is it that couples never speak about it before they get into matrimony!

I mean, I keep hearing about the usual questions people ask one another when they first start out – what are your hobbies? What kind of music do you like? What are your favourite books or movies? Do you like the sea more or the mountains?...

How is it that we miss one of the most obvious questions – what do you think about kids!

Agreed that it is not a comfortable question to ask when meeting someone on a date or even meeting someone the arranged way; in fact, it's one of those 'ostrich' questions which we feel will cease to exist if we don't talk about it!

But the more I talk to my friends and acquaintances, the more I realize that such difficult situations could have been avoided if only the couples had spoken about it earlier.

In Sneha's case, she decided to leave Rajdeep, because she felt she was at a certain age and since she desperately wanted a child, there was no other option left for her.

A sad end, indeed, to what had started out as a happy love story and could have ended as 'happily ever after'.

But like I said before, when it comes to relationship, things are never that simple. I couldn't help wondering later about the situation, had they decided to actually discuss it earlier and he had made his position clear!

Would they have fallen apart then? Would they have thrown away all that they had together?

Would they have called it off on an issue that lay so far ahead in the future?

This is actually a tricky place to be in. And the only people who can take a call are the two people involved in this decision. Only they are the best judge of whether they want the partner more or parenthood.

It's true that people change with time and age; and so does their equation and the relationship itself. But is it advisable to overlook certain obvious signs in the hope that things might change in the future?

This is what happened in Aditi's case. When she was seeing Kunal, she was well aware that he was not keen on children at all.

"But I was sure that this was his view at present. Once we are married and settled and have a nice life together, I was almost sure that he would change his mind. Even if he didn't, I was sure that I would convince him to change his mind," she said.

However, when the time actually came for the big question – to have kids or not – Kunal was unrelenting even with the passage of time.

That was when Aditi found herself in a very tight spot.

Since Kunal had been very upfront from the beginning about his position vis-à-vis children, she could not blame him for her situation.

"I was totally shattered. I tried my best to make him change his mind, but he just wouldn't listen.

I was also very hurt that I didn't matter to him that much or he would have tried to look at things from my perspective," she said.

But Kunal had his own reservations which he had been rather honest about from the beginning.

He said he never found the responsibility of kids very appealing and he wanted to live his life without what he called 'emotional baggage'.

Since he had never kept her in the dark, Aditi had no choice but to take a call about what she wanted more – him or her child.

She finally decided to stay on with him and give up her idea of parenthood. "I can still imagine life without a child which has not been born yet; but I couldn't imagine a life without Kunal, who means a lot to me," she said.

However, experts say that in such cases one of the side-effects is bound to be resentment for the partner.

"That's true. Every time I would see a couple with a child, I would feel depressed and resentful. I must admit that there were moments when I would feel really bitter that he had deprived me of the right to have a child. But then I also had to accept that the decision to get married, and then to stay with him had been mine and mine alone," she said.

That's why counsellors feel that some issues, which are likely to have a bearing on the couple's married life in the future, must be discussed while there's still time, no matter how uncomfortable or unpleasant it might be.

CHAPTER 12

IS YOUR PARTNER ADDICTED TO PORN?

THE FIRST TIME Pragya realized that it had been too long since she and her husband Jiten had sex, she had no idea that something was wrong.

"We were both too busy with our work, since I recently had got a promotion and had more responsibilities at work, and he was also too preoccupied with the new office he was setting up for his new business. That's why, it never crossed my mind that something was amiss because we both were too tired by the time we came to bed," she said.

Reality hit her when one day, she missed her flight and came home. He happened to be in the washroom, but his laptop was on and there was heavy porn playing.

"I was shocked at first. I thought maybe it had opened by mistake because he would open up several websites to research on products for his new enterprise – at least that's what he had told me when he would be busy with his laptop for hours on end," she said.

She then took a chance and checked his laptop's history and realized that he was heavily into porn. His history was full of it.

"I almost threw up in that moment. I felt disgusted, hurt, angry, and bitter – all at the same time," she admitted.

For Pragya, the shock was so much that for days she wouldn't speak to him, till one day she finally found the courage to confront him.

"He said he had been feeling too much under stress and wanted some kind of release and distraction. He then told me that he had approached me a few times but I had refused since I was too tired and had lot of work stress. Frankly, it made me angrier that he was trying to blame me for his pervert addiction," she fumed.

The tension between the two became so palpable that it seemed impossible to stay together.

"I couldn't bear to be in the same room, knowing that he was jerking off to some heavy porn all the time. I felt so cheated that all this while when I thought he was busy working, he was busy making a fool of me by devouring those pornographic movies," she said, almost in tears.

On his part, Jiten felt she was over-reacting and failed to understand why she was feeling so hurt and angry.

"I enjoy porn and so I watch it. What's wrong with that? Why is she making such a big deal out of it?" he asked.

Things actually came to a point where Pragya felt she could not stay with him.

"I just couldn't bear to have him touch me after knowing where he was getting his arousal from," she said.

It was at this point that they decided to see a therapist.

After extensive sessions where she shared her feelings of disgust, betrayal and anger and he shared his viewpoint of just looking to relax and de-stress and nothing more, the two decided to resolve things with some counselling.

The two decided to make time for one another despite their busy schedule.

"We started actually keeping a day aside a week to begin with, so that we could have sex, and he promised he would stay away from watching porn," said Pragya.

While in this case, Jiten would look to porn for stimulation, in some cases one partner is not even looking for real fulfilment – only virtual, and that's the reason for their porn addiction.

This is what happened with my friend's neighbour Rashmi. She had been noticing that her husband was losing interest in sex and she couldn't figure out why.

For days she was disturbed by the fact that maybe something was wrong with her. She kept wondering if the problem lay with her - till she discovered his collection of porn videos in his 'favourites' on his laptop.

When she confronted him, he told her that he had started looking at porn when he had come to the new city on his new job.

Before she joined him – and that was almost two years ago– he would feed on porn because he said his testosterones were playing havoc with his body.

He also realized that it had become a problem when he felt no desire to sleep with his wife any more.

"He told me that his libido fails completely when he gets into physical intimacy mode in real life," Rashmi said.

When my friend told me about it, I didn't know what to say.

"It looks like a 'real versus reel' issue," I said.

Experts say that for a porn addict, watching the act becomes the driving force; the desire to experience it, becomes secondary.

In this case, my friend and I could only suggest that Rashmi gets her husband to see a professional, because if he didn't, then the marriage was definitely facing a dead end.

However, there are times when a partner moves to porn because he or she sees it as an alternative in absence of real sex.

Take the case of Nishtha and Pradip. When they had a child, Nishtha took a long time to recover since hers had been a Caesarean delivery and some complications had risen.

Because of heavy medication and sleep deprivation she was totally off sex and Pradip would not even expect otherwise, seeing her condition.

That's when he discovered porn and it allowed him the release he was missing with his wife.

When she discovered it a few months later, he told her that it was only something he indulged in because he knew she was not in a condition to get physically intimate.

Nishtha realized that there was nothing more to it.

"At one level it came as a relief to me to know that he was unfaithful and cheating on me with a virtual woman and not a real one," she joked.

Similarly, porn addiction is not always a very serious issue. Sometimes it also stems out of sheer boredom.

This is what happened with Maushmi and Sharad. Since they had a long-distance marriage because of their different jobs, it would be months before they actually met and could be physically intimate.

It was during those periods of waiting that Sharad took to watching porn, since, as he says, he had 'nothing better to do'.

In his case, it did not interfere either with his life or his sex-life, since the moment Maushmi would come, he would not feel any need for porn-surfing anymore. In fact, he even told her about it, after which she would sometimes watch it with him, 'Only to get in the mood'. Sometimes, a casual healthy approach to your partner's porn addiction is all that is needed to help him or her get over it. The more open a couple is about it, the less complicated it is likely to get for the relationship.

CHAPTER 13

ARE YOU TAKING YOUR PARTNER'S WORK CASUALLY?

ONE OF THE recent offbeat movies that I enjoyed a lot was 'English Vinglish' and with the beautiful Sridevi as the protagonist. The story was beautiful, simple and touching with an element of honesty in it. But what struck me most was the handling of the issue of trivializing a partner's professional pursuit.

In the movie, the actress plays a homemaker who is also a small entrepreneur, who makes and sells laddoos from home. Her partner, though enjoys her laddoos a lot, does not think much of her home-run business.

The protagonist lives with the sense of resignation, inferiority and resentment due to her partner's attitude towards her work.

The same is echoed in the movie 'Chak De' where the female hockey player decides to leave her celebrity partner – vice-captain of the India national cricket team – because of his attitude of undermining her career.

The story only goes on to reinforce what many couples often have to deal with in the course of their married lives.

I couldn't help but recall a piece of news I read about an American television personality Judith Susan Sheindlin, popularly known as Judge Judy, who is also an American prosecution lawyer and former Manhattan family court judge. Judge Judy divorced her first husband, Ronald Levy, because she felt he did not take her work seriously and considered it a 'hobby'.

Though that was in the 1970s, it seems not much has changed.

Today, dual-career couples are more of a norm than an exception, with both partners having the same parameters of professional involvement.

This includes the same number of working hours, working days and the same level of commitment to their respective field of work.

But what does one do if the partners fail to accord the same importance to their partner's work as they do their own?

Well, it's a sure recipe for not just resentment but an open-ended conflict.

This is what happened with Ritesh and Shreya. When she got a job with a business portal, she was really excited because she enjoyed the job she was supposed to do.

But trouble started when Ritesh would expect her to take leave at the slightest of pretext.

"He would always call me and tell me that my father-in-law had to be taken for a check-up, or his brother-in-law was coming so I should take half-day leave. I mean, is that what he thought of my work! It was obviously not important to him. Every time I told him he could also take leave and do the needful, he would say there were too many important meetings and it was just not possible," she said.

"I started feeling betrayed by Ritesh for the way he treated my work. I felt insulted by the way he behaved when it came to my career. He just didn't think it deserved any attention, because of that I felt a huge chasm forming between us," she said.

The worst was when she had to go to Dubai for a conference and it happened to fall at the same time as their 10th wedding anniversary.

"He just scowled and sulked, saying that our anniversary was not so important to me and that I preferred to go for an unimportant event instead. He even asked me to opt out, because he felt it was not so important and when I refused, he wouldn't speak properly to me for days. I was shocked at how insignificant he considered my professional commitments," she said.

Experts say that in such situations, it is likely that the disgruntled partner nurtures ill-feelings, which manifests itself whenever an opportunity arises.

"I would try and put him down at family gatherings or get-togethers. I would deliberately not pay attention to him and pretend it was nothing. But it was always on my mind to pay him back," she said.

It would often lead to arguments, which would often spiral out of hand, with her spilling out her resentment.

"I don't understand why she can't see that my job is more important. After all, I am the one who earns more and runs the family. Her salary is only her pocket money and I have made that clear.

And so, what's wrong if I expect her to pitch in when one of us is needed at home?" he says.

While it's common to attribute gender stereotypes to such an attitude, the fact is that it is no more restricted to men.

Take the case of Som for instance. When he lost his job and started taking up freelance work, he mostly worked from home.

Though, the work required equal amount of time and focus, his wife Rati felt otherwise.

"Just because I worked from home, she would treat it as unimportant. Her whole attitude used to be almost like if I happened to be home, I have all the time in the world. She would actually make a list of things she wanted me to look into, like getting the maid to cut vegetables, ask the cleaner to come, submit the bills, call for groceries...it was almost as if being at home meant I was free," he complained.

What irked Som the most was not really the home chores but her attitude towards his work.

"I agree that it didn't pay me as well as her job did. But it was still my work and I had a certain commitment to fulfil. But the way she behaved, it made me feel like my work was unimportant.

Every other day she comes back with the complaint that I was home and yet I couldn't take care of the chores," he said.

Counsellors say that when partners don't value one another's profession, it leads to cracks that are very difficult to mend.

They add that this lack of respect towards a partner's vocation will erode a relationship since the partner on the receiving side sees it as an attack on one's worth.

"Every time she complained about the things I failed to get done even when I was at home, I felt like she was indirectly targeting me for being at home. I started feeling like she was using these occasions to drive home the point that she was wearing the pants. After all, I had just started out on my own and it would naturally take time to pick up. I expected her to be supportive of my pursuit, but she was in fact losing no opportunity to throw her weight around," he said.

Sometimes, this attitude of not valuing your partner's work enough also reflects itself in the decisions about their lives and their future.

This is what happened with Mohit, a banker and Tara, a painter. Mohit would travel a lot because of his work and he never thought much of his wife's choice of career.

"For him it was just a hobby and he also sounded rather patronising when he spoke to others about my work, almost like he was talking about a child. I felt really denigrated. Just because I stayed home and took care of house work, he thought there was nothing much to my abilities," she said.

It was only when Tara received an invitation to participate in a painting exhibition out of town that the fissure surfaced.

"He said I couldn't go because he would be away that week for an important conference and someone had to be home with the kids. It did not matter to him that this amazing opportunity meant so much to me. I tried to get him to work something out but he wouldn't hear of it.

Ultimately, I had to decline the offer but I could never forgive him for it. Things between us have not felt the same since then. If he can't support me in achieving my dream, it's not really a relationship worth working on," she said.

Experts say there is more to sustaining a relationship than just being together. It is important to also respect one another and value each other's choice of career and support them as partners.

These days both partners contribute to the family income, even though the proportion of contribution may differ. But that's beside the point. In a relationship, what counts more is not really the money but the emotional support that the partners provide one another in their professional growth, and the commitment it requires.

That's the only way the relationship can survive and take the partners towards their personal growth as well.

CHAPTER 14

ON DIFFERENT TRAVEL TRACKS!

"I HAVE FOUND out that there isn't no surer way to find out whether you like people or hate them than to travel with them."

I don't know whether Mark Twain had couples in mind when he said that, but I for sure have come to realize how apt it is for people in relationships.

When Jayant and Ami decided to go for their first vacation together (the honeymoon didn't count, since they said they were too much in love and with hormones on overdrive to notice anything else), they were really excited.

But trouble started brewing from the time they started planning the trip.

While Jayant wanted to stay in a five-star hotel, Ami felt there was no need to spend so much 'just to sleep'.

"I found it really annoying that she considered a good place to stay a 'waste of money'. I mean, I cannot bear to stay at a place where the room has a stale smell, or the sheets don't seem clean and the bathroom doesn't have all the facilities, the breakfast not up to the mark. It actually made me question myself, whether I knew her well or not," he said.

Ami on the other hand, had her own justification.

"What's wrong in my approach? I mean, we will practically be out the whole day. All we need a place for, is to park ourselves, our luggage, have a quick bath and leave. The priority is to see the city, not to spend time at the hotel. So how does it matter where we stay?" she said.

While they managed to reach a compromise and picked a four-star hotel to stay, it took the shine out of the trip for both of them. Neither could understand the other's point of view and because of this difference, every time they travelled, they would have disagreements over the issue.

At one level, it's quite normal for people to have different ideas about travelling. After all, no two people are identical. And yet, a certain common ground is necessary if two people decide to travel together.

Sometimes, these differences are not always about money; it's also about experiences.

Take the case of Shweta and Binoy, who enjoyed travelling. But while Shweta enjoyed the journey, Binoy's focus would always be on the destination.

That often led to severe arguments between the two and more often than not, the trip ended with both of them sulking.

Even the food on the way was often an issue.

"I loved stopping on the way at local dhabas and gorging on their parathas with white butter, dal makhni and lassi, but Binoy would not hear of it. He wanted to eat at a proper restaurant or a hotel, where he could have his 'healthy' meal," she said.

Counsellors agree that if a couple are not on the same page when it comes to these supposedly small issues, it could blow into bigger issues within no time.

In this case, Shweta would totally resent when he refused to eat at a dhaba and just sat there with his Bisleri bottle, and he would feel the same when she sat quietly sipping her coffee while he ordered his meal and ate it by himself.

And then, there are some couples who just don't share the same passion and excitement about travelling as their partner.

This may not be one that makes or breaks a marriage, but it sure brings in a lot of resentment in the relationship.

This is what happened with Myra and Rajan, who felt completely differently about the idea of travelling.

While for Rajan, travelling was a passion, for Mina it was a least interesting idea. Rajan thought that they would travel together very often, but they never responded to it the same way.

"For Myra, the idea of travel meant checking into a five-star hotel, watching TV, ordering room service all day long, and going for a swim or indulging in the spa at the hotel itself. She was just not interested in exploring the place or the local cuisine. It was really frustrating. I felt despondent and trapped in the situation," says Rajan.

"Even when we travelled by road, she would go off to sleep, waking up every now and then to ask how far we were from the destination. It felt so depressing to be driving by myself, listening to music and seeing a bored, sleeping partner next to me. I almost felt I would have been better off alone," he confessed.

Experts caution that such differences in approach towards travelling can breed a lot of bitterness, which over a period of time, can also lead to serious differences.

In this particular case, Rajan stopped asking Mina to come along. He would instead plan trips either with his friends or by himself.

Initially Myra was happy about it, because she hated the "whole effort of travelling" but what she didn't realize was that gradually it led to the two of them drifting apart.

Counsellors say that there are times when it's actually too much of an effort to do something which one dislikes. But a balance needs to be worked out so that the distance doesn't become unbridgeable.

In such cases, they suggest that a couple must work out some trips where they can go together.

And preferably somewhere they need not be forced to go. That way, they will have the best of both worlds, without any resentment and distance leading them to change tracks midway in their married lives.

The more I heard of such cases, the more I realized that such "travel differences" have an impact on inter-personal relations between partners, which may seem unrelated but springs from the resentment over the issue.

Partners may start snapping at each other for no reason; they may pick up arguments over trivial issues and even blame the partner for unrelated things.

According to experts, such behaviour is all about 'displaced anger'. They suggest that sometimes it's useful to explore if there is any particular reason for the partner's travel issues.

Having an honest conversation with the partner can sometimes prove an epiphany not just for you but for the partner with the issues as well.

This is what happened with Roshni and Mohan, who always fought over the expenses every time they travelled.

"He just would not let me spend. Whether it was taking a cab, or shopping, or even eating, he would scrutinize every detail before going ahead. I felt like I would explode," she said.

But one day, when she realized that she could not go on like this, she spoke to him about it very frankly.

That's when he told her that he had grown up in a very tight-fisted family and being cautious about spending came naturally to him.

That candid conversation not only helped Roshni understand the root of Mohan's attitude, but also helped Mohan in realizing that while times and situations had changed, he was still living with the fear of his past.

"That's when I proposed that we alternate the funding of our trips. I said I would fund the next two trips and he would have to do nothing except accompany me. The next two he can take care of, the way he is comfortable with. We tried it out with a little planning regarding the expenses, and since then, we have had trouble-free travels so far," she said.

Making a relationship work is never easy. But what makes it easy is the knowledge that you two want to make the relationship work.

Therapists say that sometimes a couple needs to find a middle path where both partners need to pay a little attention to the needs and concerns of the other.

For me personally, it's a total waste of money for someone who has spent so much of time, effort and energy, and it has failed to provide the couple with that break, the rejuvenation and the memories that made them plan the trip in the first place.

As wise men say – a trip with a sulking partner does not a great travel make.

And so, if you are really keen on getting back on track with your partner about travelling together, then plan out a strategy where both of you feel that the trip was worth the effort and the money.

It is never a good idea to relinquish your wish to travel with your partner; the key is to work out the right balance between the expectations that both of you have.

The very idea of travelling together as a couple – especially for a holiday – is to have fun and take a break from the routine of daily life.

It's indeed a valuable opportunity for couples to spend intimate time together and have that special bonding which often eludes one as we deal with the daily grind of life.

But what happens when the holiday turns into a combat zone with partners ending up on opposing sides?

This often happens when travel plans come under strain because of differences regarding the choice of destination.

This is what happened with Prachi and Manish. When they both got a bonus at work, they decided to invest that on a holiday.

But their very first disagreement took place on deciding on a destination. While Prachi wanted to visit Europe, Manish was keener on Southeast Asia.

They argued a lot before reaching a compromise.

"We finally agreed on Europe first and Thailand next," she said.

But sadly, that was just the beginning of differences. Things again heated up because they wanted to stay at different hotels, eat different cuisines and even see different places.

"I agreed to let her have her way by deciding on Europe, but she wanted everything her way.

Why should I have to give in all the time? It was my vacation as much as hers?" Manish protested.

Prachi on the other hand, felt he was making everything an issue.

"I felt he was making everything an ego issue. Just because he had agreed to where I wanted to go, he wanted to push his case for everything – including what to eat, where to go, what to buy…It was almost as if he wanted to prove a point," she said.

By the time the vacation ended, things had reached a point where the two realised that they had lots of differences to bridge.

Experts say that vacations are also a testing point in relationships since it is only when couples travel together that they spend a lot of uninterrupted time, with no break or away-time. It is almost like walking on thin ice, which may just crack under pressure.

While in the case of Prachi and Manish, travelling together led to the couple drifting apart, in some cases, it has the reverse impact.

When Ananya and Karan decided to take a trip to the mountains, they were both excited – especially because this was the first time, they were going to be spending so much time together in their few months of marriage.

What Ananya forgot was that she used to suffer from motion sickness as a kid. And when they were on their way back by road, she started feeling uneasy. For a while she thought against telling him, wondering how he would react.

"But when I couldn't take it any longer, I told him. He immediately pulled over and took me to a restaurant, where I threw up. He patiently waited outside the washroom and ordered a lime juice as soon as I could sit. I felt really touched by his concern and his attitude.

"That day I felt I had made the right decision in marrying him. I felt safe and loved and I fell in love with him all over again," she said.

That's why, just as living together under the same roof is very different from dating one another, travelling together is also very different from knowing one another. A partner's travel habits or behaviour while travelling tells you a lot – not just about the partner but also about your relationship.

Sometimes, the strength of your bonding is put to test when you are away from your comfort zone and into the unknown. And unless the unknown is handled properly, it is bound to affect your interaction with your partner. But once we learn to negotiate that, we can actually manage to create memories together. Bon Voyage!

❍

CHAPTER 15

ARE YOU 'LIVING TOGETHER SEPARATELY'?

I WAS THRILLED when my friend Mona announced at a get-together that she was all set to get married.

Naturally it was followed by squeals and screams and congratulations as we all hugged her and extended our good wishes.

After all, she was finally getting married to her college sweetheart Vinay, after a lot of opposition from his family over caste issues.

The two had been seeing each other since college and had managed to stay in touch even when he moved to another city after getting a good job.

That's why, as soon as the congratulations were extended, someone from the group asked her if it was going to be a long-distance marriage.

"Oh yes. We are going to live together, separately," she quipped.

"For how long?" asked another.

"I frankly have no idea, but as of now, I think this will be the arrangement. I mean I have a great job here and he has a stable job in Bangalore. Neither of us is keen on quitting at the moment and moving to another city, and it will not even be a good idea because I will not find good media jobs there and he will not find his kind of job here," she said.

"Will you be okay with living separately? I mean, how will the two of you spend time together?" asked another friend.

"Well, we have thought about it and worked out a plan. Some weekends I will fly down and on some, he will come to Delhi. We will manage," said the bride-to-be, with a brave smile.

It was a lovely evening and we were all thrilled because she was very happy. But when I went back home that night, I couldn't help but think how agile relationships had become.

Not so long ago, such an arrangement was not just frowned upon but also looked at with a lot of sympathy.

But today, due to jobs and financial necessities, the concept of 'living together-apart' and 'living separately together' (whichever way, one preferred to look at it) has become more of a norm than an exception.

Take the case of Smriti, who had a well-paying job in Mumbai. When her husband Ashish got a dream job in Delhi, Smriti realised she didn't want to make the big shift.

"I had a comfortable life here. My son is happy in the school here and I have most of my family members here as well, which for me is very important. My job here also provides me with a substantial medical insurance and other perks. I just felt I would be making a mistake leaving all that and moving to a place where I may or may not get a job with all these perks," she said.

In this case, the good thing was, they were both on the same page and hence there was no conflict over the issue.

He was going to join a start-up company and was aware of the uncertainties it entailed.

"We were both aware of the risk involved in this new venture. It would have been silly to get emotional and leave stability behind – especially when we had to consider the number of expenses involved. Our son's increasing fees, the home EMI, the car insurance and the EMI as well – we couldn't ignore all that. It's a good thing that we felt the same way about our situation and are fine with living apart for some time, till things get stable," he said.

Since both partners had discussed the issue in detail, there was no heartburn or resentment over the decision to live apart.

It took them some time and effort to stay connected but finally they managed to stay closely in touch over Skype and WhatsApp, even though they were physically apart.

According to counsellors, an open communication is the key to things working out smoothly when they have to decide on living separately – and yet together.

The commitment to not drift apart, despite the distance, is what is most important in such cases.

"We were very sincere when it came to staying in touch. When we decided on a time to connect, we would stick to it, no matter what. It was almost like we had an important appointment that we both had to keep. That really helped a lot. I think because we stayed in constant touch and communicated sincerely, we made sure that distance did not affect our relationship," said Smriti.

There are times, however, when friction creeps in between couples living in two different places.

When one partner has to deal with daily issues and problems single-handedly, it often casts a shadow on the relationship.

This usually is more likely when the decision to live apart is a compulsion or a necessity than a choice.

This is what happened with Shamima and Ali. When he found a handsome paying job in Qatar, he decided to move.

"The plan was to shift for a few years and return after I had made enough money to buy a house in Mumbai. I asked Shamima to stay in in Mumbai because our son was in school and my parents are quite old and it was not possible for them to shift. I was aware that Shamima was very upset about the decision, but frankly I had no choice, and I tried to make her see it too," he said.

While Shamima knew that his job abroad would help them financially, she was quite distressed about being left behind with all the responsibilities.

"I was the one who had to deal with all the problems here – be it taking my in-laws for check-ups, or taking my son for his tuitions and other activities, or dealing with bills or the landlord or managing the household chores by myself. It hardly felt like I was married. I felt like a single parent with the added responsibility of ageing in-laws, who were not very adjusting," she said.

What added to the problem was that every time Ali called, Shamima would bombard him with her list of complaints. As a result, he stopped calling as often as he did, which further led to them drifting apart.

"What could I do? Every time I called, she would ask me to come back. She kept saying that she didn't need the money and that she wanted me back no matter what. But that was not practical and I had no choice but to start avoiding calling her," Ali said.

What Ali did was, take the easy way out and this is what therapists would call a cardinal sin.

According to them, the lack of communication between partners especially when they are living in different places is most damaging for a relationship.

Not only does it lead to miscommunication and detachment between the partners, it also breeds negative feelings of resentment, bitterness and sometimes even jealousy that stems out of trust issues.

This is what happened with Shamima as well. As his calls to her became infrequent, she started imagining things and no matter how much he tried to convince her to the contrary, she felt that she couldn't trust him anymore.

"How and why should I believe him? He is far away from me, where I can't see him, see who is with and he doesn't even call me that often anymore. He has a whole life and a whole world away from me and I am aware every moment that I am not a part of it. I just can't trust him anymore. I feel cheated and betrayed by him," she said.

What intensifies the issue is the feeling of loneliness one goes through when living apart.

"I missed having him close to me. I missed holding him and being held by him. I felt miserable spending night after night alone in my bed and I missed having him make love to me. I felt it was cruel that he left me alone at the prime of my youth and I was acutely aware that I was not getting any younger," she said.

There is no doubt that there is nothing like having one's partner close and in the flesh, where they can touch one another, hold one another, talk face to face and lean into each other whenever the need arises.

This is why the marriage vow of "to have and to hold" seems so beautiful, poetic and romantic.

But in a long-distance marriage, this aspect of a relationship is what one misses most.

However, while this is not a desirable situation, therapists say that the impact can be minimised by ensuring that you surround yourself with reminders of your partner, which provide you with certain feelings of togetherness and proximity.

The best is to have pictures of 'shared memories' which the partners can keep going back to – something that Sonal and Manish always did.

Sonal was a doctor with a government hospital, which offered her a secure job and a secure pension. That's why when her husband was posted to another city on a three-year project, she decided not to join him because of her job.

"But one thing that we never compromised on was our time together. We made a schedule of together-time and adhered to it with sheer commitment. We would meet at the appointed hour and just chat – about how the day was, how we were doing, how were things and so on. If nothing, we would end up playing Sudoku or crossword!" said Sonal.

"We also rejigged our expenses to make space for our travel plans, so that we could visit each other at every opportunity available. That way, we never stayed apart from one another for too long," Manish said.

The two also made sure to make their meetings special – by planning dinners, outings and lots of photographs.

"Our living separately almost started feeling like extended dates, and when I got back home, I would keep going back to our pictures together – which served as a reminder that despite the distance, we were still very close and in love," Sonal added.

This in fact, is the key to making long distance relationships work for couples 'living separately Together'. To pass this test, a couple must keep the three Cs in mind - connection, commitment, and communication.

If that is in place, then it will actually turn out to be a case where the 'distance can make the heart grow fonder'!!!

❍

CHAPTER 16

ARE YOU BOTH NOT ON THE SAME SEXUAL PAGE?

IN 2014, A man in India was granted divorce by a family court over his wife's 'excessive and insatiable desire for sex'.

The first time I read about it, I was flabbergasted. For me, that was a first.

But when I read the report further, it also mentioned that the man felt 'harassed' by her sexual demands.

That actually got me thinking.

We have grown up hearing and reading about how 'good sex' boosted the relationship, with some features even stating that the number of times a couple had sex was a barometer of how and where their relationship stood.

And then this!!!

But the truth is, where at one level, a couple having lots of sex acts as a relationship booster, at another, difference in libidos can have a totally opposite impact.

Take the case of Kunal and Prakriti. When they got married, Kunal had no idea that Prakriti was just not interested in sex.

"When we went for our honeymoon, she would love to dress up and she looked amazing. She was even fine with kissing and touching, but when I tried to get into the act at night, she would look most uncomfortable. That made me equally uncomfortable myself," he said.

Initially, things went on that way, with the couple having sex once in a while.

But trouble started when Kunal, who was a sexually active guy, would approach her and she would resist him so forcefully that things became rather strained between them.

"I had to ask her if it was me, or was there a problem with her, or was there someone else! I mean it was indeed a torture for me every time I tried to sleep with her. I even asked her to see a doctor but she insisted she was fine and accused me of being a pervert and a sex maniac," he said.

Such a vast contrast in sexual desires will obviously have an impact on the relationship, because both the partners are equally affected by it.

The partner with the higher sex drive feels cheated, frustrated and gradually even suffers from low self-esteem at being sexually rejected.

On the other hand, the partner with the low sex drive feels too much under pressure, helpless and is also likely to suffer from a sense of anxiety at having to ward off sexual advances from their partner.

In some cases, it can turn out to be rather serious, as it did, in the case of Kunal and Prakriti.

One night he said he was in the mood and she as usual was not.

But Kunal forced himself on her and she fought him back so badly that there were physical marks on both of them.

The next day she left for her parents' home and filed for divorce on account of physical and sexual cruelty.

While in this case, a disparate libido level was a personality issue, in some cases such a situation emerges with time.

This is what happened with Mahua and Makrand. The two had a very sexually active life in the first few years of their marriage.

"It was crazy. We felt we could not have enough of each other. We would make out in the drawing room, in the kitchen, in the bathroom and sometimes even in the car while on a long drive," Mahua said.

But things changed when they had their first child. Since it was a painful delivery, there were some complications, because of which it took a lot of time for Mahua's body to heal.

"I was under heavy medication, because of which I had severe mood swings and my libido just nosedived. I could make out that Makrand desperately wanted to have sex but I just couldn't bring myself to feel aroused," she said.

But when Mahua realized that things were not going to be resolved soon because of her health, she decided to be upfront about it with Makrand.

"I told him that I realized that it was as difficult for him to stay off sex as it was for me to get involved. Thankfully, he was very understanding and he realized the reason behind my low sex drive. He told me not to worry about it and that things would come back to normal soon. I felt really relieved and reassured and I think I not only began to love him more but also started respecting him more for the way he approached the problem," she said.

For Makrand also, the open communication came as a relief.

"I am very active sexually and the way things stood between us, I started fearing if this was the end of the road physically for us. But when she spoke to me about it so candidly, I felt at ease, knowing that she was also worried about our dwindling sex life. That made me believe that it was a temporary phase, and I was willing to wait it out because after all, I love her and we have had a wonderful sex life together so far," he said.

While in this case open communication helped take the pressure off a potential crisis, in some cases, the option is not really available.

This is what happened with Mukul and Pari. When he lost his job and she started taking on more work to make up for the single income, one of the things that suffered was their sex life.

"I would come home really late and even then, there was so much of office work left, that I had no time and energy left for anything else. I could see it taking a huge toll on our relationship but someone had to pay the bills," she said.

But Mukul would often feel disheartened by the fact that with the loss of his job, the sexual chemistry between them had also taken a beating.

"I couldn't bring myself to discuss it with her because every now and then when I would make some physical overtures, she would turn around and say that with so much of stress about maintaining their lifestyle and managing the expenses, sex was the last thing on her mind. It not only put me off, it also came as a blow to my self-esteem," he said.

But what he really missed were the small physical interactions that the two of them shared in their married life.

"We have both been very physical people, and we loved hugging, touching one another, holding hands and sometimes even stealing a peck on the cheek or the lips to show our affection to one another. But now, that had completely stopped and this really affected my peace of mind. Now when I made an effort to touch her, she would shrug me off, saying she was busy, or not in the mood, or had to attend to something. This change in our physical behaviour is what I fear will be the death knell of our relationship," he noted.

Experts say that these small physical gestures between partners keeps the relationships alive.

Sex is important in a relationship no doubt. But what's equally crucial is to stay physically connected, since that creates a bond between two partners that makes the quality of sex far richer than anything else.

In fact, it is not just small physical interaction that is significant for a strong sexual relationship; it is also the whole attitude towards foreplay and after-play that also defines the quality of a couple's sex life.

Many women are said to need foreplay to get in the mood, and when that is missing, it instantly reflects in the quality of sex with their partner.

This is what happened with Vinita, who was facing a lot of issues with her husband Sushant in their bedroom.

"I hate it when he just pulls me to bed and starts making love. I need to feel in the mood as well. And if I tell him that, he scowls and tells me I am making excuses. It has often led to a lot of strain in our bedroom," she said.

The same is the case with after-play. I have read endless features of how women hate it when the men "roll off and sleep" after love-making, while women crave much more.

None other than Billy Crystal observed the difference between how men and women approach sex and all that's attached to it when he said, "Women need a reason to have sex. Men just need a place."

This is what Sakshi experienced with her partner Mohit.

"We would have amazing sex – something that I would relish and look forward to. We would have mind-blowing orgasms every time we had sex. But what took the shine off it was that Mohit would disengage as soon as we were done, and it left me feeling slightly uneasy. I felt like he had no more need for me and I felt discarded. I would often tell him that I need him to hold me, cuddle as after-play, but he just couldn't understand that," she complained.

Mohit on the other hand, would get irritated by her constant need for after-play.

"I failed to understand why she was so hung-up on after-play. I mean, the fact that we both had remarkable sex and multiple orgasms weren't enough for her? I have no energy or desire left to cuddle her, or hold her, but that's because we were both satisfied. This thing of after-play is getting on my nerves now," he said.

But therapists say that post-sex contact is also quite important in a relationship, since it helps build a strong bond between the couples. Experts concur on the subject, saying that couples who indulge in after-play reflect far more physical satisfaction and intimacy than those who don't.

For women especially, after-play is an expression of being desired and loved.

Sometimes, lack of after-play can start affecting sexual intimacy between partners as well, as it happened with Sakshi and Mohit.

Because of the way she felt after Mohit just 'abandoned' her after they had made love, she started refusing and making excuses.

"I will not allow myself to be treated like a sexual commodity. I feel he comes to me only because he needs physical satisfaction and most of the time, I feel it's not me he wants; it could have been anyone under him. That's how he makes me feel after we are done," she said.

Things got so strained between them that they started staring at divorce. After a friend suggested, they decided to see a counsellor.

"I love her but I don't have any energy or inclination left after I have had an orgasm. And much as I tried to make her understand that she is the only one I desire and feel completely sexually satisfied by, she wouldn't listen," he said.

However, after a few sessions, he started holding her close and sleeping, and was surprised to see that for her that was enough.

"I couldn't believe that we were about to drift apart for something so small and even beautiful. She didn't expect anything else from me except that I hold her close, snuggle and sleep together.

Strangely, once I started doing that, I found myself loving her more than ever, and our sex life also reached a level higher than before," he admits.

Some couples who are aware of the role that both 'foreplay and after-play' play in the relationship also take it to another level and sometimes even experiment with it.

It could be just cuddling or spooning or even just sleeping with your head on his chest and his arm around you; or it could be something as exciting as taking a shower together after love-making.

It's a sign off that will make the experience of sex richer in quality and leave both the partners feeling not only fully satiated but also loved, desired and valued.

❍

CHAPTER 17

ARE YOUR PARTNER'S MOODS GIVING YOU THE BLUES?

WE ALL HAVE our good days and bad days, phases of feeling high and low and all of this naturally reflects in our mood, our attitude and our interactions.

Most of the time, we figure out ways to deal with it, how to come to terms with it and somehow manage to ride over it.

But it's fine as long as you are the only one bearing the brunt of it. However, things change when two people get married and another person becomes an integral and intricate part of not only one's life but moods as well!

I have often heard people argue about sharing things, finances, work or space. But not many have realised that two people in a relationship share not just feelings and thoughts but end up sharing moods as well!

Not many of us have ever thought about it. But the fact is that in an intimate relationship, it is very natural to be affected by each other's moods as well.

For better or for worse, when two people are so closely connected, moods are as infectious as laughter, cold or a yawn.

By virtue of being together, partners become vulnerable to feeling more or less the same as the other partner.

This can work both ways. If the partner is irritable or sad, it is quite possible to end up emulating the feeling, regardless of whether we have a reason or not.

That's what happened to Anushree when her husband Jasbir went into depression after he lost his job.

She would motivate him, help him look for new jobs and even heard him out when he went on a self-pity mode.

"I really did my best to act normal and positive. I also told him not to worry because at least one of us had a stable job and finances were being managed. But every time I sat with him, I found him completely negative – not just about his professional life, but life overall. I understood what he was going through, but to listen to it day in and day out, started taking its toll on me. I knew things were going downhill when I realised, I was being sucked into that swamp of depression myself," she said.

Counsellors say that in cases where a couple is deeply attached to the other, such 'spousal mood infections' are quite common.

Proximity makes the partners vulnerable to the change in each other's moods, vibes and feelings, and they unconsciously start reflecting the same.

But it's not just the negative moods that affect the partners. There are times when positive moods are just as transmittable.

This is what happened with Suman and Rishi.

"We were in the middle of planning our anniversary celebrations when my boss informed me that I had to travel out of town for a conference. We both couldn't leave town at the same time because we had an ageing parent to look after. We could manage a break of a few hours because of the attendant but leaving the city together was out of question. I was really down in the dumps as my balloon burst. But my husband started saying it was no big deal and that we could still plan a grander party once I got back. With his peppy mood, I started feeling less depressed.

That's when I realised that his positive mood actually succeeded in lifting my spirits," says Suman, who works in an event management firm.

But since mood infections can be good or bad, certain safeguards needs to be kept in mind to insulate oneself from the risk of being affected by your partner's moods.

Experts say one of the most important things to keep in mind is to 'detach' yourself a little. It may not be an easy task, but it's not difficult either.

This is what Mansi would follow every time she felt her partner's mood was going to pull her down.

"I would just make some excuse and leave the house; till the time I felt his mood would be negative. I told him I needed to take the dog out for a walk and just left him to deal with his mood. As for me, the fresh air, the walk and just being away from his moody self, worked wonders for me. Earlier I would stay around, try to change his mood and end up feeling miserable myself. But later I decided I needed to take care of my mood first and if anything was going to spoil it, I would rather disengage for some time," she said.

It actually worked for her and saved her from catching the 'mood infection' – on account of love and responsibility.

"I have come to understand that my first responsibility is towards myself and my mental well-being. Unless I am mentally fit and strong, I will not be able to help anyone – least of all, my partner. That's why, when I sense a situation where I might end up in a bad or negative mood myself, I just try and extricate myself. That way, I don't end up resenting him or sulking, and he somehow manages to get over his bad mood, when there is no one to fan it," she laughs.

Experts also say that it's important to be able to identify mood triggers in one's partner. This can help the couple in actually facing the reasons behind the change in moods and then resolve the issue.

This is what Mona did, when she noticed that every time her best friend came home, her husband would end up in a bad mood. After series of arguments and phases when the two would end up fighting every time she came to visit. Mona sat him down to ask him what bothers him about her and puts him in a bad mood.

"He told me that he found her very aggressive and felt she was always inciting Mona to be equally aggressive when it came to her married life and spouse. He said he felt insecure since he felt the friend had a lot of influence on Mona and he feared that it would start affecting their, married life. I assured him that for me she was just a friend from the past and nothing she said affected me. Once I reassured him, he stopped behaving like a pressure cooker when my friend visited," she said.

Therapists also emphasize the need for patience and a degree of understanding if the partner suffers from moods swings. It's very normal as the first reaction to confront and end up having a fight when one of you is having a mood swing. But what's important here is to understand the reason behind the behaviour. If it is related to an issue, then it's best to talk about it and resolve it – nip it in the bud as they say.

But if it is a personality disorder or related to some illness or depression, then it's a good idea to encourage them to seek help. But whatever the reason, if the moods are affecting your married life and casting a shadow on your peace of mind, then it's best to communicate with your partner, with full support and understanding.

❍

CHAPTER 18

WHEN 'WHAT TO WATCH' PAINTS A GRIM PICTURE!

I RECENTLY CAME across an interesting piece of news while reading a magazine that almost made me cough while in the process of having my leisure cup of tea. The news item read: "A Japanese woman has divorced her husband because he 'didn't really care for' the movie Frozen. The anonymous woman was apparently unable to be with someone who couldn't appreciate the greatness that is Frozen, citing his opinion on the film as 'grounds for the divorce'."

Can you believe that!!!

And you all thought movies were just about entertainment!!

Well, not any more. It is increasingly becoming a make-or-break issue in a relationship, where the couples either bond or drift apart when it comes to movies and their preferences.

Some time ago, my colleagues and I were generally talking about movies at work, when one of my colleagues said he happened to go for a recently released multi-starrer movie, which left everyone totally shocked.

He was someone who held such tear-jerker movies in utter contempt, so naturally we pounced on him for his 'change in taste'.

He was honest enough to admit that he still stood by his choices, but added that he was forced to go for the movie under the pressure of his newly-married status, since it was his new bride who was keen on watching the 'drama'.

So, had he turned into a hubby who pandered to his wife's every wish – no matter how distasteful it was to his palate?

"Definitely not. If I decided to go with her for that sloppy movie, it was because I made her agree to come for 'The Avengers' in return, though she hates these superhero movies. I think we are seeking revenge through movies," he said, as we all burst out laughing.

While this was a funny way of putting it, the truth is that very often different tastes in what we like to see or listen to, often matters a lot in a relationship. It is one of those things where opposite tastes don't attract!

Take the case of Jaya and Sanjay. When the two got married they were happy to discover that they were both very fond of music and movies. It was because of that that they were also on the same page when it came to investing a bomb in getting a great Bose music system home and also a home theatre.

However, they realised that there was a problem in their paradise when they discovered that their taste in what they wanted to see was very different.

"She enjoyed those black and white movies and I just couldn't bear to see those. I found them really slow, dull and boring. And she hated the science-fiction and action movies that I loved.

She said she couldn't bear to see all that 'maar-dhaad' (action) and called them cacophonic and nonsensical. But I go ahead and watch it whenever I feel like. I mean, if she doesn't like it, she need not watch it. It's as simple as that," he said.

It was simple no doubt. But the fact is, if couples started watching movies alone very often, then togetherness will eventually take a beating.

"I would actually sit down and still watch those action movies with him because I felt at least we will be sitting together. Otherwise, we hardly get any time together. What hurts me is that he never takes my choice into consideration. It's almost like – watch it or leave it. I mean, if I have to spend time with him, it's I who has to compromise and concede. He will never sit with me and watch the movies I like. Why should I be the only one wanting to spend time together? Is that only my responsibility? I have also started doing the same now. I also watch my kind of movies on my laptop or my phone and during that time I am totally incommunicado. If he doesn't need my company, I don't want his," she said.

But counsellors warn that when couples get into this 'you watch your movies; I will watch mine' trap, the relationship is definitely affected.

Trouble starts when the supposedly small issue of entertainment spills over into other areas of their relationship and life. The pent-up resentment often finds a vent in other issues.

"I used to be so upset at his selfishness that I started taking it out on every small pretext. I would ask our cook to make the kind of food I liked – spicy and rich, when I knew he preferred less spicy with less salt. But I stopped bothering about what his preferences were. If he didn't care about things I liked and didn't, then I am not obliged to consider his likes and dislikes either," she said.

But while point-scoring is fine in such cases, it is the relationship which starts heading towards a breakdown, with such an approach to dealing with the conflict.

One of my friends Radha came up with her own approach to deal with such a situation.

"My husband Ravi hates going to movie halls. He says he finds the place suffocating and is also unable to sit still in one cramped seat for three hours. He says flights are a compulsion but he won't inflict such a torture on himself voluntarily," she said.

He offered to get her a good home theatre but for Radha, it was not the same experience.

"I enjoy the whole process of going out, being in that throbbing crowd, watching the ads, the trailers while sitting in the seat in anticipation of the movie...I love everything about it. I just don't get that sitting at home and watching it even if it's on big screen," she said.

And so, she decided to do two things. She would either make plans with her girl gang to go for movies, or sometimes, if they were busy and there was a movie she didn't want to miss, she decided to go solo.

"The first time I did that, I felt miserable initially, and hated my husband and my friends for ditching me. But believe it or not, I soon realised that some people may look at you slightly curiously for some time, but then they stop paying attention. The society is changing to some extent I feel, and now when I go alone, I just don't feel awkward anymore," she says.

Well, to each his own. If she had found her way of dealing with the difference, then kudos to her.

"I do feel slightly upset with him once in a while, but then I realised I would rather go alone and enjoy the experience than take a disgruntled partner along, who is not only miserable himself, but ends up making me feel miserable and guilty as well. Togetherness, at that cost, is not a good idea for me," she laughs.

But counsellors admit that not all couples are fine with such an arrangement and they insist on making sure that their choices and their preferences are not overlooked at all in the theatre of their relationship.

In order to ensure their equal rights, and maintain the level of democracy in their married life, my neighbours Ankita and Sourabh managed to reach a compromise.

"We decide that we will allot alternate weekends to one another's movies. One weekend, we will both watch my kind of movies, and the next weekend we will watch movies of his choice. That way, we both had our say and we both watched it together. Gradually, we realised we started liking the other's genre of movies as well," she said.

While in this case, the couple was open to compromise, reach a consensus, and save their relationship from a potential conflict, others are not so adjusting, especially when it comes to everyday routine of watching what's on TV.

Believe it or not, several couples have often fought bitterly over what to watch on television.

Counsellors have often warned that seemingly innocuous issues like whether to watch news on prime-time television or soap operas or sports match, can draw battle lines between the partners.

This is what happened with Akshay and Mahima, who found themselves in the middle of an argument every evening, when they returned from work and sat down to watch some television while having dinner.

"It may seem silly but it was something that really made my blood boil. I think it was really unfair that I had to come back home and watch a whole bunch of people screaming and shouting at one another for hours at a high decibel. I mean, after a long exhausting day at work, if I wanted to watch something light and entertaining before going to bed, was I wrong?" she asked.

"I also had an equal right to watch what I liked. But no, it was always either news or sports – which I had no interest in, but I was the one who had to endure it all. He would scowl or just leave if I put on a channel with some songs or a movie. Every evening would turn into a battle," she said.

Experts warn that such fights, if not resolved soon, can end up turning into a power game.

Take the case of Shreya and Manas. Between the two of them, Shreya was the one who managed the household expenses since she had a fatter pay cheque – something that was mutually agreed upon.

But the area where the difference in financial status in the power game manifested itself was in front of the TV.

She would always insist that I change the channel to what she wanted to watch. It was not something she said but clearly implied by her actions. I often ended up watching the news online, but it made me feel quite bitter to see how she was using her monetary prowess to get her way," he said.

Of late I have actually come across some couples who have decided to have two television sets at home, because neither wants to give in.

But counsellors caution that even though such an arrangement may work for some time, the hidden cost may be high.

Even in such a situation, one may hold a grudge against the fact that he or she has to watch it in the other room, while the partner gets to see it in the comfort of their bedroom.

As for the distance between the partners, I may be wrong but I do fear that there is a strong possibility that separate TV sets may just be the beginning of the end.

Today, it's separate TV sets, tomorrow, it could be separate rooms and soon, it may lead to separate lives. Who knows!

That is why therapists strongly advise couples to talk about it and express their hurt, their concerns and even their fears about where this might lead.

Sometimes, we fail to see the obvious. But with an honest discussion, the brewing crisis may be averted and the partners may get a 'better picture' about the situation they are heading towards.

That's why when I heard my couple friends – Surya and Mini – and their solution to this predicament, I was impressed to say the least.

"What we did was to work out a rota of sorts, of odd and even days. On odd days, we would watch the shows I liked, and on even days we switched to the shows he preferred. That way, we both got to see our shows without any resentment," Mini said.

"We also started recording our favourite shows and watching it as and when convenient, after discussing which should be seen and which could be recorded," Surya added.

Now that's what I call a hit show!

Not only did they succeed in reaching a mutually agreed arrangement, but also ensured that they got to spend ample quality time in front of the television set as well, with healthy communication and understanding.

❍

CHAPTER 19

ARE PETS AN ISSUE BETWEEN YOU TWO?

THE FIRST TIME I read about a woman in Bangalore, who decided to turn down a marriage proposal because the guy did not like her dog, I was both amused and impressed.

My friends and I laughed about it and some even debated the issue, with 'those who loved pets' on one side and 'those who disliked pets' on the other.

But while this was a case where there was no relationship to really end, in several cases, such divergent attitudes towards pets can lead to serious problems.

Take the case of Rashmi and Suraj. When the two got married and took up a separate apartment,

Suraj was very clear that their pet dog, Bonzo, would continue to stay with them.

Even though Rashmi was not very comfortable with the idea, she felt it was not such an issue that needed discussing beforehand.

But gradually, things started souring between them over Bonzo.

"I hated the fact that he would allow Bonzo in bed with us. Imagine making out on the same bed on which a dog has just been! I couldn't really get in the mood with the thought of dog hair on the same bed. I also had a lot of problem with the strong odour that Bonzo left on the bed and in the room. It naturally affected my mood and he would get really upset about it," she said.

For Suraj, the issue was not just Bonzo; it was something far more serious for him.

"She was always aware that I am really close to my dog. He means the world to me. And every time she created a ruckus over his smell, his presence and his hygiene, it made me really mad! I felt like it was a direct attack on me, because for me Bonzo is not 'like my family'; he is family," he adds.

In some cases, it's not just the hygiene issue but even the finances involved, which may not go down very well with the partner who is not that into pets.

This is what caused a lot of friction between Astha and Prashant.

"She had never been fond of pets but for me living without my dog was unthinkable. What added to the tension was the cost involved. Every time we had to travel, we had to look for a pet hostel.

She would always throw a fit over the dog boarding cost, while cribbing about the expenses doubling up because of our own travel and the arrangements to take care of the dog in our absence. It was like a pattern. Every time we had to travel - either for work or vacation - we would fight and I almost felt like cancelling the trip," he said.

Not just that, there were regular arguments over the expenses incurred over regular visits to the vet, the vaccinations, the dog walker and even his food.

"I was not ready to compromise on that account by any means and I failed to understand how she could even bring these things up. When it came to our kids, she was fine, but I hated the step-motherly treatment for my dog, which was no less than my own child for me. It also changed my entire perception of Astha as a person," he adds.

The issue led to a lot of strain in their relationship.

"For him, it was a case of love me, love my dog but what he couldn't understand was, for me, managing the kids, my office, the house and then the dog, became too much. I also resented the fact that with the expenses skyrocketing with such high school fees, the tuition fees, their future and their incessant demands for mobiles, games, extracurricular classes, sports, I felt constantly strained financially. On top of this, accommodating further expenses on account of the dog seemed unnecessary to me," she said.

Owning a pet has been the source of conflict for many couples. Some partners feel that they can deal with inanimate issues such as compatibility, ego, finances and animate issues like children, finances or even relatives, but when it's about another living thing such as owning a pet, they find themselves out of depth.

Take the case of Kishan and Smita. Since Smita had dogs as companions throughout her childhood and teens, she craved to have one even after she got married. But Kishan disliked dogs and said it was out of question. They would often argue over it and gradually it turned into a major ego issue.

"He was aware of how much having a dog meant to me. I had tried convincing him by telling him that having a dog around made me feel calm and even kept my blood pressure under control. But it made no difference to Kishan. He was adamant about not having one in his house because he had no love lost for them," she said.

They still don't have a dog and continue to have a normal married life, but Smita still has those phases of depression and resentment and inwardly blames Kishan for being insensitive to her needs.

Counsellors warn that sometimes these small disagreements or resentments over something trivial like 'pets' gets blown out of proportion because it starts reflecting on other aspects of the relationship which needs to be addressed.

This is what happened with Nina and Akshay when they got married. Nina was passionate about dogs and could not live without them. But Akshay was just not comfortable with the canines at home.

"I have never had dogs at home and that's why I am not comfortable with sharing my space, my time and my partner with a dog. I hate it when Nina pays more attention to taking the dog out for a walk, cooking for him, playing with him and taking him to the vet than to me. Sometimes she refuses to accompany me for late night parties with friends or social-dos, because she can't leave the dog alone for too long. At such times I feel resentful, even jealous, that I don't feature anywhere in her scheme of things," he said.

It's of course true that if the couples share the love for dogs, things are totally different, as in the case of Debu and Mahima. They were both dog-lovers and would often work together on the cause to save stray dogs.

"It really helped that we were both on the same page when it came to our feelings for dogs. The day I came home with a stray pup I rescued; I was unsure how Debu would react when I told him I would like us to keep it as our pet. But he was fine with it and we have been taking care of the dog together since then. For me, the fact that he and I think and feel alike on the subject, makes me feel really secure and relaxed. I also feel that our bond has become stronger since the incident. To know that your partner is as committed to the cause you feel so strongly about is a beautiful feeling," she adds.

Counsellors say that ultimately, relationships are all about accepting and accommodating one another's viewpoints.

It's not possible to have the same opinion about things and people and in this case - pets. But what is possible is to find a balance between accepting something if it matters a lot to one partner.

It's indeed a thin line between accepting and standing one's ground. But in this case, it's the partner who dislikes dogs who has a more difficult decision to make. That's why couples must sit down and state clearly why they are for or against the decision to have a pet. Either way, whatever the partners decide, it must be a mutually accepted one, so that there are no hard feelings or simmering feelings of resentment.

Only sincere and honest communication is the key to a happy relationship, and in this case, it's imperative to ensure that there are no 'pet issues' to contend with in, your relationship.

❍

CHAPTER 20

WHEN YOU CRAVE "ME TIME" INSTEAD OF "WE TIME"

"Some people ask the secret of our long marriage. We take time to go to a restaurant two times a week. A little candlelight, dinner, soft music and dancing. She goes Tuesdays, I go Fridays."

- Henny Youngman

WHEN I GOT a call from my school friend Rajni, who has been out of touch for decades, I was naturally surprised, and even a little sceptical.

My first thought was - why the need to suddenly reconnect after so long!!!

With those feelings I agreed to meet her for a cup of chai.

As soon as I saw her, I could see that she looked a pale shadow of herself.

She seemed to be doing well she said - had a good job, a stable family life, a nice husband and two sweet kids.

I had no idea how time just flew by. She was really excited as we raced down the memory lane.

We were in the middle of our "do-you-remember" session when she suddenly said, "I feel so alive and rejuvenated. I am really enjoying this break from Kushal," she said with a sheepish laughter.

Before I could say anything, she started off, saying how she missed her 'me-time', which she said was in short supply ever since she got married.

"But why's that?" I asked.

She let out a long sigh.

"The thing is, my husband Kushal, is really nice and I have no complaints really. But the truth is, he doesn't let me do anything alone. It's always – let's do that, let's go out, let's see that...I like that, but I also want to do a few things alone, like go out with my group of friends sometime, attend some classes on my own, watch my kind of movies without any guilt..." she seemed set to go on and on but stopped with a sigh.

I was slightly surprised so to say.

"So why don't you? Does he stop you?" I asked.

"No, he doesn't stop me, but he doesn't encourage that either. I mean, he can't understand why I want to meet friends alone, why I need to go for movies with them or why I want to enrol in aerobics or Zumba alone. It's always – let's do it together, let's meet them, let's go out together. I don't have the heart to tell him that I miss being by myself sometimes. I need to be alone, to be in my own world and have some me-time!" she said.

I could totally understand what she meant.

When two people get married, it is very normal for couples to spend every moment together. The whole notion of "me time" seems to go out of the window as soon as the two become a couple.

It works fine initially because the togetherness is a new feeling and a whole new experience, and a couple enjoys the emotional expansion that being in an intimate relationship brings. But with time, the need for space resurfaces.

Problems start when one partner in unable to understand the other's need for space and for some time away from them. In their perception, such a need to have some time to themselves is seen as a 'rejection'.

Experts caution that if a partner seeking some time alone fails to get that from the other partner, it can lead to resentment in the relationship because the affected partner feels 'smothered' and the other feels 'snubbed'.

This is what had happened with Rajni. Every time she told him she was going to meet her friends, he would want to come along.

"He offers to drop me and then hangs around with us. I have tried being polite but he doesn't take the hint. Recently I tried to tell him in a slightly direct way that my friend and I would rather be on our own and he got upset. He wouldn't speak to me for days. I had to finally tell him some story about how she wanted to tell me something private about her partner and that's why she was not comfortable with him. Only then was he pacified," she said.

"So how come you are here right now? Does he know?" I asked, worried that I might become the cause of yet another row between them.

"He knows. He is not too happy about it, but he is learning to live with it," she smiled.

"How's that?" I couldn't help asking.

"Well, one day I decided to join Zumba classes in a sports club close by. I really wanted some time to be by myself, have my own thoughts and my own group and my own circle of friends with whom I could have my own rapport, instead of getting along with his close group of friends.

But when I told him, he said he would join with me. That's when I couldn't take it anymore and I threw a fit. I asked him point blank if he did not trust me or he thought I would leave him, because that's exactly the impression I got and if he continued doing so, I would actually leave him," she said.

I was gripped by the whole interaction.

"My god, how did he react?" I asked.

"Well, he was taken aback but he saw that I was serious. So, I sat down and told him that I just needed to indulge in some activity alone – not because I didn't want him with me, but because I wanted some time to spend just as I liked. He was still not sure of what and why I wanted all this, but seeing my determination he is trying to accept it," she said.

Like Kushal, there are many people who fail to understand the concept of space between partners. For them, in an intimate relationship, there should only be 'we-time' instead of 'me-time'.

Some partners even feel insecure when faced with this need for some time and space alone.

What they fail to understand is that 'me-time' is just that – a time for one to spend with oneself or the way one likes.

Take the case of Shaan and Neha. When they got married, Shaan had no idea that Neha could be so possessive.

"I had a huge circle of friends – from school, from college and even my old workplaces, and I liked meeting them every once in a while. We would go out for bowling or cricket match or even catch up for beer or drinks every now and then. But after I got married, Neha insisted that I spend all the time with her and she felt disgruntled when I was not so keen that she comes along. We had major arguments about it and I felt depressed that she couldn't understand that I just wanted to be alone with my friends," he said.

Sometimes, being by oneself gives one a sense of freedom, a sense of abandon and a sense of being free of responsibility.

But what most people don't realize is that instead of posing a threat to the relationship, some time alone and some space between the partners actually enhances the relationship.

When the partner feeling smothered in too much 'togetherness' gets that breathing space, he or she comes back into the relationship with far more energy, freshness and closeness.

This is what happened with Ankita and Mukesh. When after eight years of being married, she suddenly announced that she was taking a solo trip, he was shocked to say the least.

It was not so much about the logistics, but about the fact that she needed to be away from him.

"He was hurt, upset and even confused to an extent. I felt bad that I was doing this to him, but I really needed to know that I had a life of my own and that I was my own person – one that did not always exist as a pair or as a joint entity," she said.

As for Mukesh, what left him totally bewildered was the very idea of wanting to be alone when they could be together.

"I mean, don't we enjoy travelling together, dancing together, playing sports together, partying together or drinking together…we do everything together and we love doing that. So why this sudden need to go without me? I naturally was concerned - not about her really, but about us!" he confessed.

What most couples assume when they get married is that besides being joint owners of bank accounts, bedroom, bathroom or the whole house, they also jointly own each other's time, space, social circle and attention.

Experts point out that spending time with one another should be a matter of choice – not compulsion.

Because when that happens, togetherness turns into suffocation.

"His incessant need to do things together and be together made me feel like I couldn't breathe anymore," she adds.

That's why most marriage counsellors suggest that partners must be alert to the idea of space between each other.

In absence of this understanding, marital bonds can become binding. That's why 'me-time' in between 'we-time' is a must; it acts as a ventilator between partners and keeps the relationship fresh and alive.

Take the case of Shikha and Ajay, who were aware of the need to allow the other person space to be themselves. That's why they were able to capitalize on this and make it work for them.

"When she goes to meet her friends or for shopping, I don't insist on tagging along. In fact, I enjoy that time to do my own thing, play my video game or meet up with a friend at a pub. By the time she comes back, I have done my own thing and I look forward to her company once again," he said.

Therapists also suggest that it's healthier to do certain things alone if the other partner is not really inclined.

"I find the idea of shopping and shunting from one shop to another quite tiresome. And so, we spoke about it and came up with a plan. I told her that while she went shopping with her girl friends, I could take care of the kids. And when I have to meet my friends for a drink, she would manage things. The only thing we would set limits to, was how many hours we are going to be away. I inform her when I will be back and she does likewise. That way we both are mentally free to enjoy our own time without having to deal with a sulking partner," he said.

No wonder experts vouch for the fact that if the couples understand the need to be independent of the other sometimes, and not feel hurt or offended by 'me time', then the relationship will have enough breathing space for the relationship to be healthy and become far stronger than ever before.

❍

CHAPTER 21

ARE YOUR PARTNER'S PET PEEVES GETTING ON YOUR NERVES?

"I love being married. It's so great to find one special person you want to annoy for the rest of your life."

– Rita Rudner

LOVE IS A beautiful feeling no doubt. But it's amazing how it takes so much more than just love to sustain a relationship.

Small habits, traits or quibbles that you wouldn't have even noticed earlier, start irritating once couples start living together or spending too much time together.

These 'pet peeves' are like that buzzing sound that one barely hears initially, but one which over a period of time, starts irritating your senses.

It can be something as small as burping loudly even after being told several times or it may be the habit of leaving a whole bottle of water out of the fridge after just taking a sip.

Now I know what you are thinking. Do such small issues even matter in a relationship!

But the fact is, these pet peeves can actually short-circuit a relationship.

Take the case of Meher and Jay. While there was nothing wrong in their relationship, Jay's pet peeves were a constant source of annoyance to Meher.

"I would always tell him to let me know by when he would get back home or inform me if he was getting late. But he would always tell me he would be there in ten minutes and would take almost an hour or two. There were times when he would tell me he would be back by 5 and I don't see him till 8. Now wouldn't that make me furious?" she would ask me.

I couldn't help but agree. It's not that she was keeping a tab on him or was a nagging wife who needed an account of his every second, but it affected all her plans.

"All I wanted was a clear picture so I could plan my chores accordingly. If I know he is going to be home after about two hours, I could sit down to do my ironing or check my office mail and answer them or even clean up my cupboard - or any other chore which is pending. But because he never tells me clearly, I am left sitting and actually waiting for him, doing nothing worthwhile. Initially, he would laugh about it, pacify me and then try and make up, but over a period of time, I started feeling resentful. It made me feel like he had no respect for my time," she said.

These small issues may not be big enough to warrant a separation or a divorce, but they are still the sand particles that end up acting as irritants in the fragile base of a relationship.

Take the case of Prabhat and Arti. Since both were working, it was decided that they would divide work and take care of certain tasks.

Among other things, Prabhat had said he would wash his own clothes as and when he was comfortable. But it always irritated him when she would be at it, asking him about it.

"At first it would be about when I plan to wash the clothes. Now I have my own way of dealing with this chore, but she would not let me be. It was always - when are you going to wash it; when are you going to iron those? Are the clothes going to lie around in your basket? When you going to put them in your cupboard and so on! I felt hounded and even though I told her I would take care of it, she would turn around and tell me if this was my way of taking care of it. I felt like turning around and telling her - these are my clothes, my cupboard and my house. I can do whatever I like with it. But for the sake of peace and harmony I always keep quiet, but on the inside I end up fuming," he says.

Sometimes, incidents, which may seem funny at the outset, seem to be anything but, when one finds oneself at the receiving end of your partner's pet peeve.

This is what happened between Akash and Jia. Every other day Jia was faced with a situation where he would enter the bathroom for his shower just when she entered the room after clearing the kitchen and packing up.

"I hated that I had to sit and wait outside the bathroom for him to come out. It was so unnecessary. I couldn't understand why he couldn't get in earlier and finish with his chores while I was busy clearing the table and putting things away. But even after telling him politely a few times, he would get up exactly when I was done with the work and was heading toward the washroom. I was not only angry but started getting bitter as well. I felt he was deliberately doing this because he either wanted to irritate me or he was just not bothered about the fact that I also had to have a bath and be in bed on time, instead of sitting outside with my towel and nightwear like I was in a hostel," she said.

While it did not blow into something serious, it did affect Jia's relationship with Akash and started reflecting in her attitude towards him.

"I stopped making tea for him when I made one for myself. Or even when I would heat the food, I told him to take it himself. I would almost wait for him to react so that I could give it back. I just wanted to get back at him," she said.

While Jia's actions were not going to break the relationship, some other pet peeves may not be that harmless.

One of the most common pet peeves that men often complain about is the phrase – 'I am fine' when their spouses are anything but.

Take the case of Myra and Shreyas.

"Whenever I sensed there was something bothering her, I would keep asking if she was alright. And her reply would always be - I am fine - even though I could see she was not. It really irked me to have to keep pushing to find out what the matter really was. I wanted to shake her and tell her – "Just be out with it", but I had to go through the rigour of persisting before she came out with what was wrong. Not just that I hate it when she gets up in the middle of an argument and walks off, leaving the whole issue unresolved. And since I don't have the energy to start the whole process again, I just leave it there. Then there's the 'silent phase' where she stops talking and answers in monosyllables when I try and make an effort to act normal. At such times I feel like banging my head against the wall," he says.

But it was a habit that stayed with her and even though Shreyas put it down to her personality type, it didn't stop annoying him.

In fact, there are other personality traits which can be classified under those 'pet peeves' which drive one crazy.

Behaving in public is one such bugging habit which many couples find difficult to handle without offending the partner.

This is what Ajay had to contend with at get-togethers or social gatherings, when his wife would start discussing politics.

"She has no clue about politics and its intricacies, but she still insists on commenting on the developments. I find it really embarrassing and I don't know what to do about it. If I were to tell her she would take umbrage and then I will end up pacifying her. But I feel really awkward when I see people reacting to her obvious lack of political knowledge," he said.

I have heard several people tell me, that as long as the pet peeves are within the four walls of their room or even their house, it's still manageable. But things get really uncomfortable when the outsiders are involved.

Take the case of Arzoo, who had a lot of trouble dealing with her husband's pet peeve of always interrupting her.

"I could still handle it at home by getting up and walking away in a huff, but it vexed me no end when he did it in public – before friends, relatives and sometimes even strangers. I remember this one time when one lady was asking for directions and I started telling her how to reach there since I pass that area every day. But the moment I started, he just interrupted me and started telling her himself. I felt really peeved. That's not all. Every time I start narrating something to my family or friends, he will interject it with his comments, or his version and I end up letting him share the incident than be constantly interrupted. I know he doesn't do it deliberately or mean it as an offence but I still get really annoyed," she says.

Experts say that pushing the issue under the carpet is not a solution if it continues to irritate you and gnaws at the back of your mind.

It's true that talking to your partner about their pet peeves may not always be easy, as you can be accused of 'overreacting' and 'being overly sensitive' but if it's upsetting and breeds frustration, it is necessary to talk about it so that it doesn't eventually snowball into serious differences.

What one can do is to tackle it gently and not use a confrontational approach. Sometimes, just making your partner aware of their pet peeves can do the trick. And asking them if there's anything about you that annoys them, can actually seal the deal.

And then again, sometimes it's all about perspective as well. Think about it and ask yourself if your partner's pet peeves are really that detrimental to your relationship.

A habit of leaving socks on the floor, wet towel hanging at the back of the bathroom, cold water bottle left outside the fridge and many more pet peeves may be annoying but that's about it. Sometimes it's important to ask oneself if it's a fight worth fighting or just letting it go with a long sigh.

Take your call.

❍

CHAPTER 22

NOT 'SPORTING' ENOUGH!

I RECENTLY HAD a moment of epiphany when one of my friends, Roshni, who happened to be visiting, suddenly sat up in the middle of channel surfing.

"Don't tell me the football season is set to begin!" She said with a tone, which I felt almost bordered on the shrill.

"Uhh yes! And since when have you become interested?" I couldn't help asking.

Roshni was one person in our whole class who was as fond of sports as a convict is to the noose.

She hated sports – or any form of exercise to be precise – and it had earned her the nick name of 'couch potato'.

"I would rather be a couch potato than jumping jacks like you people," she would retort.

So naturally I was shocked to say the least, to see her sudden interest in sports. But I was immediately corrected.

"Of course, I am NOT. I am just concerned about my married life – and my sex life as well - going for a toss now," she said as she sank back in her bean bag.

I didn't know whether to laugh or be concerned for her!

"What's the connection?" I asked again.

"Well, the connection is that there is a total absence of connection between us when his football season begins. He behaves like an animal when the game is on. He screams, shouts, curses and I am almost always on the verge of pulling my hair," she said.

Seeing my amused expression, she said, "I am not kidding. It drives me crazy to see him going 'yes' and 'ahhhhh', only to realise it's for those screaming players on screen and not while in the act with me," she said as I burst out laughing.

"Really don't get it you know. So much of adrenalin rush from watching other sweating men. Is that normal?" she asked me, as I doubled over laughing.

The complete contrast in their taste for sports couldn't have been more obvious. But while I was under the impression that the issue was an innocuous one, I was mistaken.

Often, this seemingly innocuous issue is seen to strike a relationship hard.

Take the case of Roshan and Mira. Every time the cricket World Cup started; the couple found themselves on a sticky wicket.

"I always dreaded the cricket season. During that period, Roshan would just not pay attention to me or help me with any housework either. It pissed me off that I was expected to take care of everything at home, while he would plant himself before the TV every evening as soon as he got back from work. I would also be tired after work but he would leave everything – from buying groceries, vegetables to deciding what to cook and then clearing the kitchen while he would just not budge from his seat," she complained.

Often this would lead to arguments between the couple and soon things came to a point where they stopped talking to each other.

"Really couldn't understand what her problem was. I mean can't I enjoy watching my favourite game in peace without being taken on a guilt trip? She would create so much hype about dinner, kitchen, work, and all this after I told her I would gladly order from outside and she can also put her legs up and relax. But no, I had to be given a lecture every five minutes on all the work that had to be done," he said.

The problem in this case didn't seem to be cricket or work or food. It was all about not having the same level of interest in sports – in this case, cricket.

The fact is, most marriages are seen to feel the ripples when the couples have few things in common. Among the prominent ones on the list is, being poles apart when it comes to interest in sports.

Sometimes the issue ends up being so sensitive that it ends up threatening their relationship itself.

Experts say that the issue is not so much about sports and their lack of interest; it's more about lack of respect for your partner – about his/her likes and dislikes.

"In fact, this is what bothered me more. I never interrupt her when she is watching Sex and the City or The Big Bang Theory or anything else that she is heavily into. I expect the same consideration when I watch my favourite game," Roshan said.

Therapists say that it's not important to like the same things as your partner because two different individuals may naturally have different interests.

But what is important is to not undermine the interests of your partner.

It may not be possible to develop similar tastes but what is indeed possible is to work out a way where neither encroaches on the other's space to indulge in their interests.

This is what Medhavi and Tushar did about their different tastes. Since Medhavi was really interested in playing squash and Tushar had no interest in the sport, the two worked out a plan to ensure it worked well for both.

"When Medhavi told me, she had joined tennis classes on weekends, my first instinct was to complain that weekends were our only time together. But I realised that she had no choice because the classes were held only on weekends. That's when we decided to make it work for us.

Every time she went for her classes, I made myself a nice drink and caught up on my favourite WWF, which she hated since she could not tolerate those aggressive fights. By the time she returned, I had had enough of WWF, and we were more than happy to be with one another. I actually felt that since both of us had our space to indulge in our favourite sport, we were more indulgent with one another," he says.

Such adjustments hold the key to a successful relationship. Counsellors say that couples need to be crystal clear about one thing – and that is, no matter what, they want the marriage to work.

If they are clear about that, then it becomes easier to work out ways to ride over the differences and score the winning goal.

Take the case of Tara and Ishaan. When Tara realised that Ishaan was crazy about tennis, and for her the sport was like Greek, she decided to do something about it.

She was aware that he used to play tennis in college and was training professionally until an injury forced him to opt out. But his passion for the sport remained intact.

"I loved to see how engrossed and involved he was while watching the game. I decided to get involved as well, so that I could be part of a world that he felt so strongly about," she said.

She read up on the sports and tried to get a hang of it and then she started watching the game with him, asking him for stuff on it alongside, which he was more than happy to provide. "I felt a lot of love for him, seeing the way he tried to educate me about tennis and in a strange way it brought us closer," she said.

Ishaan couldn't agree more. "I realised that she was doing this only for me and I felt really touched by her efforts and also by the fact that she attached so much importance to what mattered so much to me. I developed a lot of respect for her as a person and as a partner after that," he said.

That's why counsellors say it's important for couples to not make the issue of interest or disinterest in sports an ego issue. Simply put, for one partner, sports may just be a game; but for your partner, it may be nothing less than a passion.

The trick is to accept it as just that and respect it. Never play spoilsport in the relationship by showing a lack of respect, lack of consideration and lack of understanding towards what matters a lot to your partner. Only then can you make it as a winner to the marital finishing line.

❍

CHAPTER 23

SPARRING OVER PARENTING STYLE!

ONE OF THE things I have grown up hearing is that having children is important because it strengthens the bond between the couple and makes them come to one another.

After all, the child belongs to both and since the responsibility is a shared one, it's but natural for them to join forces in child rearing.

But alas, there are also cases when instead of bringing them together, parenting sometimes ends up driving them apart.

Sadly, sometimes rift between partners starts the moment they become parents. Differences over what and how much are partners doing for the new-born baby, especially when it came to chores, food and overall involvement.

This is what happened with Rhea and Somesh, when they had their first baby.

"It was very difficult for me. Suddenly my life had turned topsy-turvy. I was sleep-deprived, tired and faced bouts of depression. And I hated it when I saw that Somesh's life was back to normal after the paternity leave ended. He was back at work, and life had resumed like nothing had happened, while I was constantly struggling with the baby's sleep patterns, his feeding schedule, his nappies and other endless things. I really resented that and we would have regular fights because of that," she said.

Somesh on the other hand, failed to understand his wife.

"Tell me something, can I feed the baby? I mean, is there any biological possibility for me to do that? Then what is she cribbing about? Even if I stay home – and I can't, because one of us will have to keep working – what will I do, instead of just being there!" he says.

Unfortunately, their relationship ended badly and they parted ways because Rhea's resentment grew to a point where she felt he failed to contribute anything towards being a parent.

Even in the case of Mira and Jay, it was the initial period of their parenthood that caused a major damage to their relationship.

"I used to take care of the baby throughout the day, and expected him to help me out once he was home. Even during the night when the baby would wake up, he would not budge. I would nudge him and ask him to see why the baby was crying but he would not move. It was always left to me to get up even as my eyes were slamming shut and I couldn't move, but he would just turn and continue sleeping. We often fought over it because I would shove him off the bed or shake him up and wake him and ask him to help. After all, the baby was his too, and I was shocked at how he couldn't see that!"

Counsellors agree that the initial period of parenting can be quite stressful – not just for the new parents but for the partners as well. Sometimes, it can be a make-or-break situation as well, as it happened with Rhea and Somesh.

That's why they suggest that it's a good idea to sit down and chalk out a few things each partner expects from the other once they have a child. It's also advisable for couples to attend sessions on parenthood together, so that they are both on the same page when it comes to parental duties, responsibilities and expectations.

Sometimes, major differences arise between couples – simply because they don't agree on how to bring up their child.

The differences could range from what the child should eat, where he should study, what profession should he aspire for, to name a few. Or it could be about a difference in approach towards parenting – whether to be strict or lenient, controlling or liberal or be friendly or authoritarian.

And since no two people are alike, their approach towards parenting may not be the same either.

And when the couples start having differences over how to deal with the kids, the relationship comes under a cloud.

Take the case of Jagriti and Ajit. When they had their son Gautam, their joy knew no bounds and they started focusing on him like he was the centre of their life. Things were fine till he was a kid. But things changed when Gautam went to college and started becoming his own person. For Ajit, who had always decided which school his son would go to, which subject he would take in high school, which extra-curricular activities he would join, this change became difficult to negotiate. He just could not let go of control and as a result, the father and son would have regular and ugly altercations. The one person who was hit the hardest was Jagriti, who found herself sandwiched between the two.

"Ajit is very resentful that he has lost all control over his son and takes out his anger on me. I am the one he keeps badgering, blaming me for Gautam's behaviour and asking me to convey his views to our son. I could see that he was in the wrong but the moment I said so, he would accuse me of siding with the son and driving a wedge between father and son. It was too much for me to handle and I started avoiding my husband because I totally disagreed with his behaviour towards our son who was a grown-up man now and deserved his freedom to grow. But Ajit couldn't see it like that," she said.

Experts say that sometimes couples may have no complaints from one another and may even have a good relationship. But if they don't agree with one another when it comes to parenting skills, things can go downhill very easily.

They also say that if such things are not addressed in time, it can lead to cracks that can never be filled.

This is what happened with Rati and Vijay. When they had their daughter Ayana after seven years of marriage, they were ecstatic and very involved in their daughter's life. But things changed when she entered her teens.

Like her friends, Ayana also wanted to do sleepovers with her friends, attend parties and even go Travelling, but Rati was totally against it, while Vijay, who came from a very adventurous family, saw nothing wrong in that. The difference of opinion in how much freedom to allow their daughter led to regular arguments between the two.

"I failed to understand why Rati was so against letting Ayana have some freedom! I am also her parent and equally concerned about her well-being, but Rati is forever accusing me of being too liberal with her. What I don't like especially is, she keeps warning me that I will come to grief if I give her so much freedom and then I would understand. I don't think it should be about blame game – if something happens - god forbid. What we need to do as parents is to get the right balance. But Rati is just not in agreement with me on this, and her attitude is making things very difficult for all of us," he said.

As a result of their differences on parenting issues, trouble started brewing between their own relationship as well.

Ayana started avoiding her mother and became closer to her father – a fact that led to further ill-feeling between the couple. She accused him of pitting her own daughter against her, while he found himself avoiding her.

"I couldn't believe that my husband was colluding with my daughter. I felt it was really petty on his part to use me to get close to our daughter, even when he knows it's not right for her!" she said.

On the other hand, Vinay criticised Rati for alienating herself – not just from their daughter but from him as well.

"Because of the muddled way in which Rati was handling our growing daughter, I felt I was totally falling out of love with her," he rued.

Experts caution that the relationship between the partners is directly affected when they disagree over how to bring up their children.

If stretched over a period of time, such disagreements over parenting style can severely harm a couple's relationship.

That's why counsellors suggest that it is important that couples discuss issues about how to deal with children first among themselves than before their children.

Take the case of Kumar and Minal, who were happy in their relationship till their daughter started seeing a boy in the locality they both disapproved of. But instead of being on the same page and addressing the problem together, Minal would accuse him of not having spent much time on their children's upbringing, while he would accuse her of not giving the children good values.

"The issue was not about our daughter and the problem we were facing. Somehow it had exposed our own failings and resentments as partners and parents," said Kumar.

There was also a lot of blame game about who was responsible and who had allowed how much leeway to the children – all of which failed to resolve the issue and ended up causing irreparable damage to the couple's own relationship.

Experts also suggest that if the parenting approaches are very different and are affecting the relationship, then they should seek professional guidance since it may have a bearing not just on the child's future but on the couple's relationship as well.

What most couples fail to see, is that parenting is not about scoring over the other partner; it is in fact to be seen as a joint project where they are expected to do what's best for their child.

Then there is also the issue of how much time and effort a partner is investing in their children – something which often starts reflecting in the relationship between the couples.

This is what happened between Akanksha and Bharat, who had two children. While the couple had a great married life, things started going downhill when their children started growing up.

"Bharat was always busy with his friends, parties and wanted life to continue the way it had. But since the kids were now young, they needed our time and attention and Bharat was never there. I actually slowed down on my socializing, late night parties and even travelling so that I could be around the kids to support them as and when needed. But Bharat never felt the need, and he started getting upset with me when I started refusing invites to his friends' parties because our kids had their exams. I was appalled that he felt he had no sense of responsibility and continued with his life, like there was no need to change anything. I resented the fact that he did not try to get involved with the kids at all. It really affected the way I used to feel for him," she said.

Bharat on the other hand, felt Akanksha was taking her role as a parent way too seriously, which he often dismissed. According to him, the kids were doing fine and needed no hand-holding.

"My parents never indulged me like this and we learnt how to live and survive in the world without such spoon-feeding. I don't think there's any need to press the pause button on our lives just because of kids," he would argue.

Their different approach towards parenting started taking its toll on their relationship rather strongly, when Bharat stopped asking her to accompany him and she started accusing him of neglecting his duties as a parent.

"He would keep alleging that our children shared nothing with him and that I was responsible for it, and I could only gape at him. How does he expect them to share things with him when he is never there, when he never shows interest and never takes out time to be with them? It made me livid and I started going off to sleep before he came home because I felt he was not a good parent to our children," she said.

"Parenting is not easy. Just by giving birth we don't become parents. I make sure to take leave to drop them to their exam centres because they are nervous; I stay up late into the night to give them company so that they don't feel alone; I plan my weekends in a manner where I get to spend time with them and they share what's happening in their lives. You don't just become a parent by paying the fees and providing money for their food, clothes and shelter," she adds.

Things would have come to a breaking point between them, when Bharat offered a weekend away to talk about things. That's where they decided to thrash out their issues.

"I told him very clearly that if he did not get involved with the kids, he would lose them and eventually lose me as well, because the distance that would creep in would naturally have a bearing on our relationship as well," she said.

Luckily for them, he heard her out and decided to follow what she wanted him to do.

"I took them out to water parks, movies and even outstation regularly and strangely, I realized how little I knew them and about them – their likes and dislikes, what made them excited and what bored them and the discovery made me feel like a whole new person. What's more, my relationship with Akanksha really metamorphosed into something really beautiful. It was a good feeling to be working together on what she called a joint project, and if I may add, I developed a lot of respect for her for the way she devoted herself to the well-being of our kids," he said.

That's what the bottom-line is, when it comes to partners turning parents. Unless parenting is done with a consensus between the partners, they will not be able to walk away with the award for being good parents, let alone being good partners.

❍

CHAPTER 24

ARE YOU TWO LEADING PARALLEL LIVES?

FLEXIBILITY IS THE new norm today as we negotiate our lives with several complications and strive to find a 'mutually acceptable' mean method to survive.

But when it comes to relationships, one is always treading on difficult terrain.

It is usually with the purpose of living life together that a couple gets married. Its but natural.

There's no other way to either justify living under the same roof if one is not keen on creating a life together or a home together.

So how and when does that change? Have we ever thought about that?

The only thing one knows is that one never really gets to know when the partners shift tracks from being on the same path to living parallel lives. What makes it uncanny is that often it takes the partners by surprise because it happens so slowly that even the couples involved don't realize it.

It seems like just yesterday that the couples shared each and everything about their day, their feelings, and the people in their lives and even their thoughts. And then suddenly, it's all gone!

When did they move from living together, sharing the same roof, same room, and same lives to living, separate, unconnected and parallel lives?

The strange part is that the process begins slowly, like water falling silently over the rock and eroding it and eventually dislodging it just as suddenly. Because the partners have missed the signs, the relationship suddenly becomes something they are unable to recognize.

And the truth is that we often miss the very first sign of entering into dangerous territory when we first start making certain adjustments according to what seems to be the 'need of the hour'.

Take the case of Suhasini and Mahesh. They both rose in ranks in their respective jobs around the same time and the work hours increased significantly. As a result, they barely managed to see each other at home.

They would both come home at different hours and with lots of work to catch up on even at home; they barely spent time with each other. Messages about the chores, the menu and the maid were left on the fridge and on WhatsApp, and the machinery of the house somehow managed to keep running.

But in the process what came to a standstill, was their relationship and their life together.

"I didn't even realise when we started drifting apart. But now when I look back, I can see that all those times when we decided against going out together – be it movies or to a dinner because we both had work commitments, or when I started eating out because I had work in the office and he totally understood, must have been the time when we started living parallel lives," she says.

Mahesh agrees. "We were to be blamed for it actually. We should have made sure that no matter what, our relationship was most important and we needed to draw a line. I now feel miserable when I recall that so many times when she was taking our dog out for a walk, she wanted me to come along and I refused, thinking I could get some more work out of the way. She would also get angry when I failed to notice if she was wearing something new. I would make light of it at that time but now I feel sad that I could not take time out to even notice and compliment her," he admits.

Therapists say that when couples start getting too preoccupied with their own work and lives, and end up excluding the partner, they are moving towards bifurcation in their life together, even though they are seemingly 'together'.

But they warn that it is with these small concessions and compromises that the distance starts creeping in. If left unchecked and unnoticed for long, it can also lead to emotional disconnect between the partners.

This is what happened with Astha and Suraj. After they had kids, the expenses skyrocketed and they both had to put in extra effort to cope up.

They also had to work out time slots to help their kids with their studies initially. Because of which they barely got time for themselves, and before they knew it, they had drifted away to different worlds, which only connected when they discussed their kids.

"I was surprised when one day she made pudding and said she used to love it as a kid. I realized I had no idea about what she was anymore and that I knew so little about her. We hardly seemed to have any time for ourselves," he said.

Astha couldn't agree more.

"We both felt things were running smoothly and we were managing to give due attention to our work and kids, but neither realised that we had hardly managed to give proper attention to one another. I still remember how we felt good as we accommodated one another. For instance, I never stopped him from going out with his friends since I could get some work done while he was away, and he would babysit while I went out with my friends. But soon we realized that while we had made our lives easier, we really had no life together anymore. I couldn't think of the last time when Suraj and I had fun together! We seemed to have actually forgotten what it was like to spend quality time with one another and no one else," she said.

That's what counsellors caution modern-day couples about. In this era of packed and overwhelmingly busy schedules, the need of the hour is to come out with a good balance between managing work and families, but most importantly, managing the life that the couple shares.

Nothing is more important than staying connected with your partner. For this it's important that the two of you stay involved in each other's lives and be mindful of one another's presence in your lives.

One of the most simple but important things that works wonders is to take some time off work sometimes and spend it with one another.

This is what Sharmila and Bijoy would often do to keep their relationship alive and to stay connected.

Every now and then when Sharmila had some free time around lunch, she would connect with Bijoy and ask if he could meet her for lunch. It was not always possible, but whenever they could manage, they would sneak quality time out for themselves. Or when he was coming close to her office building, he would message and ask to meet if she was free.

"Those lunches have always been our favourite outings. It makes me feel really loved and wanted and valued whenever he calls me up to check if we can meet. And it makes me feel secure and very much in love," she laughs.

That's what really matters in the end. When couples manage to strike a balance between holding on to their life together and letting it all go for the sake of convenient parallel lives, will they manage to create several beautiful memories and moments together.

❍

www.ingramcontent.com/pod-product-compliance
Lightning Source LLC
LaVergne TN
LVHW041034150826
845672LV00001B/320

* 9 7 8 9 3 9 3 7 5 7 9 2 0 *